Wakefield Press

Is This the Way to Madagascar?

Born into the farming community of Caltowie in the mid-north of South Australia, Lydia Laube gained her nursing qualifications at the Royal Adelaide and Calvary Hospitals in Adelaide and then set off to see the world. She worked in Darwin, Papua New Guinea, Hong Kong, London, Italy, Indonesia and, finally, Saudi Arabia, the experience which led her to write her first bestseller, *Behind the Veil*. Lydia's story of her travels in Madagascar, *Is This the Way to Madagascar?*, is her seventh book.

 Is This the Way to Madagascar?

LYDIA LAUBE

Wakefield Press

Wakefield Press
16 Rose Street
Mile End
South Australia 5031
www.wakefieldpress.com.au

First published 2007
Reprinted 2021

Copyright © Lydia Laube, 2007

All rights reserved. This book is copyright. Apart from any fair dealing for
the purposes of private study, research, criticism or review, as permitted under
the Copyright Act, no part may be reproduced without written permission.
Enquiries should be addressed to the publisher.

Edited by Kathy Sharrad
Cover designed by Nick Stewart
Designed and typeset by Clinton Ellicott, Wakefield Press

National Library of Australia
Cataloguing-in-publication entry

Laube, Lydia, 1948– .
Is this the way to Madagascar?.

ISBN 978 1 86254 755 1 (pbk.).

1. Laube, Lydia, 1948–   – Travel – Madagascar.
2. Madagascar – Description and travel. I. Title.

916.91

*To the memory of Minnie Buchanan,
part of my life for more than forty years.*

Contents

1	Hello Sailor	1
2	Nautical but Nice	8
3	Singapore Fling	14
4	Damietta Detour	20
5	Landfall La Spezia	29
6	Napoli Nostalgia	42
7	Arrivederci Roma	50
8	Madagascar Achieved!	57
9	Mountains and Monarchs	69
10	Mad (about) abus	79
11	Bush Bashing	93
12	Mountain Training	104
13	Beating the Bank	114
14	The Meaning of Life	122
15	Blowout in a Brousse	129
16	Lemurs at Last	137
17	In Search of Pirate Treasure	148
18	Cruising the Canal	162
19	The Wrong Mr Right	172
20	Home	182

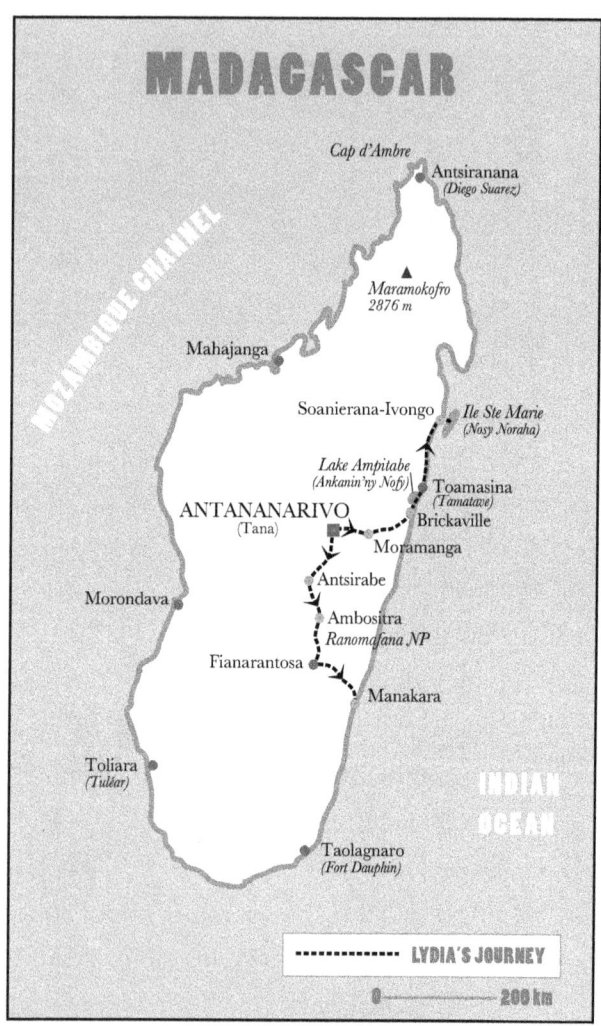

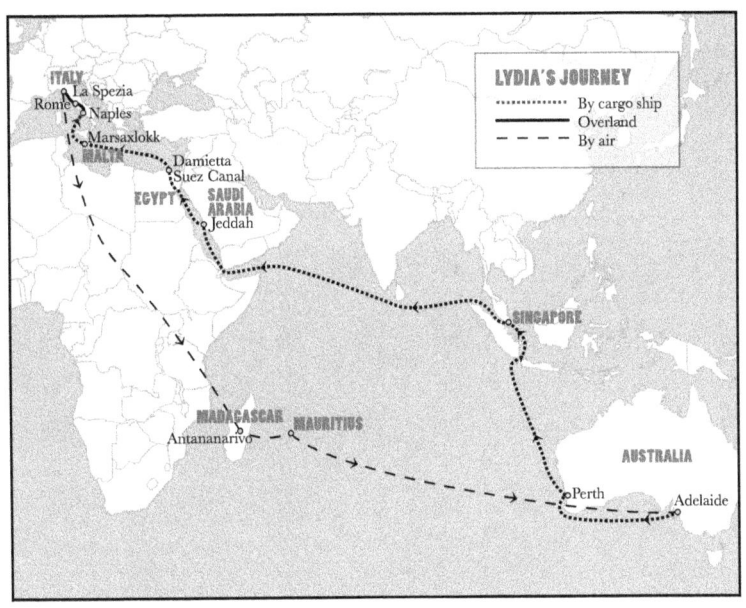

1 Hello Sailor

Scouting up and down the steel security barrier like Bugs Bunny trying to outwit the rabbit-proof fence, I eventually located the *Manet*. A large container ship, I recognised her by the red, white and blue colours of the French flag on her funnel.

At last I was about to sail from Adelaide.

I have one word of advice for all those folk who say that they would like to travel by cargo ship. Persistence! This is not a simple task. At every step of the way you will be told that it can't be done. It can. But not easily.

I started this marathon mission by phoning the shipping agents listed in the yellow pages. They all denied that any passage on a ship out of Adelaide was possible. Next I went to the internet. In London I found a travel agent offering freighter voyages. He told me I should contact an office in Sydney. The first person I spoke to there said his firm didn't do it. I asked to be put through to someone else. This individual said he had never heard of cargo ships picking up passengers in Australian ports. I persisted and was passed from floor to floor, person to person, until the fifth person I spoke to, a woman, said, 'Oh yes, we do that!'

However, after several calls back and forth with her, no ship was found going where or when I wanted. I went back to the London agent who said I should try Freighter Travel in New Zealand. Bingo. I had hit the jackpot!

So one afternoon in mid-August I finally boarded my ship – destination Madagascar. I would have to travel a devious route to get there. Not by choice, there was no other way. No passenger-carrying cargo ships cross the Indian Ocean in a direct line to Africa, so I had decided to take the *Manet* to Europe, from where I hoped to obtain passage on one of the freighters that regularly sail down the African coast and across to Madagascar. And disembarking in Italy would give me the chance to make a sentimental journey to Naples, a city I had lived in many years ago. What happened after that I left in the lap of the gods. Somehow I would reach Madagascar.

Despite the difficulty of finding a way through the security fence – Outer Harbour has become heavily protected now that the free and easy pre-terrorist days are behind us – its guardian was friendly and helpful. He inspected my passport and phoned for transport to deliver me shipside. A conveyance promptly arrived, driven by a young man who apologised for it being a daggy old van. As if I cared.

'Beats walking,' I said and, my gangplank ascent somewhat hindered by a clunky floral arrangement of daffodils that had been pressed on me when parting from the rellies, I followed the sailor who carried my bag.

'Careful, it is the thirteenth,' called down a watching seaman as I tripped over the second rung of the ladder.

'At least we aren't sailing today,' I chirped. Then I remembered – we were, tonight!

Clutching daffodils, handbag and umbrella, I grumbled to myself, terrific – setting sail on the thirteenth should guarantee that Murphy comes along too.

I made it onto the ship, handed over ticket, passport and vaccination certificate, and was taken by the lift – a rare find on a working ship like this – to be safely installed at last in what was to be my home for the next month.

The porthole of my cabin on E deck, two levels below the bridge, looked out over piles of stacked containers to the sea.

My door was labelled 'Super Cargo', which mystified me until I discovered that it meant 'passenger' – as in excess baggage. I was superfluous to the real business of this ship – freight. Left to my own devices, I was half unpacked when a seaman knocked at the door and summoned me to appear before customs.

Despite the fact that she had been dragged out on a Saturday afternoon just to clear me, Ms Customs was cheerful and smiling. Back in my cabin, my next visitor was the steward, Nico, apologising profusely for having been ashore phoning his family in Romania and not onboard to welcome me before. Nico galloped me off on a Grand Tour of the ship. It was, like my cabin, clean and neat, in a spartan sort of way.

Functional rather than plush would be an apt description of the passenger accommodation. But my cabin was large and had everything I needed: a double bed with a wooden rack above it to store my needed-for-the-night goodies, a small fridge, a desk and chair under a porthole, and a wardrobe. The floor was covered with institutional linoleum and the bathroom was identical to that of the German container ship on which I had sailed to South America – a huge shower, everything nailed down, and hand rails wherever possible.

From the porthole I watched as containers were loaded rapidly – 300 filled with wine from the Barossa Valley were taken aboard in Adelaide. Should we be shipwrecked on a desert island, we were not going to die of thirst, or, for that matter, unhappy.

Dinner at seven o'clock was rather disappointing. As this was a French ship, I had entertained great hopes for the cuisine. But the first course was a pile of semi-cooked potato salad and the second was very ordinary spaghetti bolognaise. A camembert cheese that wasn't at room temperature followed. I consoled myself with two glasses of French wine. *Vin ordinaire*, it was not as good as cheap Australian red, but was complimentary so I drank it.

After dinner I met my fellow voyagers, Mervyn and Pam, a retired English couple. They had been into Port Adelaide to eat, wise souls. I gathered they were not exactly enthralled with the on-board rations either.

Later that night I was almost asleep when, at eleven o'clock, the ship's engines started. I got up and through the porthole, watched the lights of Adelaide slowly moving away. Happy to once again lie in bed and feel the rise and fall of a ship beneath me, I soon slept.

During the night the swell of the sea increased, and by dawn, when we had reached the Great Australian Bight, the *Manet* was rolling and pitching. From my porthole I looked onto a totally grey world – a dull, leaden sea covered with white caps, under a dismal sky. I showered with difficulty, one hand gripping the safety rail fiercely, then weaved and staggered down to the dining room on B deck to see what was on offer.

The English couple had warned me breakfast would be 'continental' and a most unhealthy swill. They were not wrong. I was the only passenger who appeared for breakfast that morning – and for the rest of the voyage. I was appalled to find that bread and jam was the meal's main feature. I do not consider this breakfast. I like eggs, tomatoes, and any other edibles I can lay my hands on – leftover stir-fry, chicken legs, chops. All I received now was coffee and poisonously sugared white bread that tasted like sweetened cardboard. I gave the jam a miss.

The waves increased as the day wore on until the ship was heaving and plunging boisterously. This is pretty usual for the Great Australian Bight, which has a reputation for ferociousness. Pam appeared briefly in the passenger's sitting room. Mervyn was seasick and she wasn't feeling too flash either. Neither appeared for any meals that day or the next. Oh well, all the more for me.

I went out on deck but soon retreated back inside. Now the sea seemed like a great wild beast. Huge plumes of spray flew smoking off the top of mountainous waves, soaring past the sides of the ship. Then the captain issued a bulletin – passengers were forbidden to go out on deck. The sea had begun breaking inboard over the containers. The wind took the waves that smashed into the prow, threw them up and over the ship in sheets of water, hitting the decks as high as the one outside my cabin.

I was invited to the officers' mess for a drink before lunch, a normal procedure for passengers on Sundays. The ship's complement consisted of ten officers – two Romanian, the others French – and a crew of Romanian seamen. The officers were a pleasant, good-looking bunch – with one exception being the fat, antisocial first officer. I had heard from my fellow passengers that this gentleman thought passengers an unnecessary pestilence, and I soon gained the impression that he would, if given the chance, sell us to the first available pirates.

Another Sunday treat was that passengers sat at the officers' table for lunch and not at their usual table, a small separate one on the other side of the dining room. Were the officers being punished or I? The Sunday victuals turned out to be no better than the weekday fare. But the wine served was a good Hardy's red the captain had bought in Adelaide.

In the afternoon I tried to use the small notebook computer I had brought along for company, but this proved impossible. The chair and desk bounced about wantonly to the frenzied rock and roll the ship was performing. The captain had told me at lunch that we were in for bad weather that evening. So what was this? I wondered, as I stared at the rain and sea spray pelting the glass of my porthole. The ship was bucking like a bronco!

Dinner that night, after a solitary afternoon confined to barracks, was a toasted sandwich of the awful white cardboard bread followed by a hamburger patty that sat, alone and forlorn, on a limp lettuce leaf. The patty was thick and the cooking process had not reached its middle. My stomach wouldn't accept this offering; even my legendary cast-iron digestion baulks at raw meat. I took more wine to console it. And so to bed, as Sam Pepys would say.

I slept well although I was conscious of the sea becoming even rougher. It banged and crashed the ship around, the force of it rolling me from one side of the bed to the other. Only the guardrail stopped me from flying out onto the floor. I lay there pondering how the small ships of past explorers and adventurers had coped with a sea like this. Imagining these tumultuous waves breaking a lesser vessel than ours to bits, I felt the horror of being cast into that cold, turbulent, merciless water.

In the morning I opened my eyes to see my chair waltzing matilda-ing across the floor of the cabin. Getting up was not easy. As I stepped into the bathroom the door swung wildly on a wave, clouted me in the back and precipitated me into the hand basin; and every time I took my wary eye off it the cabinet door smacked me in the head. This ship method of travel is not for the unsound of limb – or wind, for that matter. The lift went out of action in rough weather and the stairs were a feat that had to be tackled several times a day if I wanted sustenance – the food being four decks down.

During the night, I had attacked my bed light with my head and it now refused to function (the light, not my head) but Nico fixed it promptly. He was a treasure, fussing over his charges like a clucky old maid.

At the dining table this morning I found evidence that the conditions were now considered really unstable – the pepper, salt and mustard were now incarcerated in a metal cage.

Pam, who had almost recovered from her *mal de mer*, and I

spent a marathon three hours watching *Lord of the Rings*, after she had rescued me from a frustrating half hour of trying to fathom the workings of the infernal video machine. Except for the hobbits, I didn't like the film. It was too violent. But I did learn something from it – the hobbits and I are soul mates. I, too, consider that civilised living requires first breakfast, second breakfast, elevenses, lunch, afternoon tea, dinner and supper.

The ship meals did not improve. The only good part of the repast was dessert, which was invariably cheese and fruit. It was good cheese, but twice a day every day! Have a heart! Of course, there was always plenty of wine with which to drown our sorrows.

After three mornings listening to my plaintive cries for food, the very kind Nico asked the cook to produce some eggs for me. That gentlemen flatly refused, roaring, 'Pesky bloody woman', or French words to that effect. But Nico, my mother hen, took pity on me and from then on he sneaked into the galley every morning before the cook arrived and fried two eggs for me. Later he asked the cook for some ham to add to my eggs but, judging from the bellows of rage I heard, the answer was a definitive NO. Nico told me, 'The cook said, Eggs! Eggs! Eggs! Is all!'

2 Nautical but Nice

Finally, after three deprived mornings, I had achieved a respectable breakfast and life was sublime again. After my meal I climbed up the internal staircase, two decks, to visit the bridge. This massive place, bristling with dials and charts, had a wide expanse of windows all the way around it from which a view of the ship's front and side decks, as well as the distant coastline of Australia, could be seen. On the bridge my photo was taken for the police line-up-type mug shot that had to be hung – there are those who had predicted this would happen to me eventually – on the bridge for identification purposes. When the ship was in port this photo was also exhibited at the top of the gangplank, so that no strays or stowaways could gain access. Phillipe, the ship's young cadet officer, was the photographer. He ungallantly waited to take my picture until I had stepped out on deck, been nearly blown away by the wind, and returned with my hair standing on end.

The crew welcomed visits to the bridge at any time and seemed to appreciate the diversion. It must get boring up there when there is nothing to look at except the sea. But I got into trouble with the deck-swabber. He smacked my fingers for interfering with the potted plants that lived on the window ledges. They were not allowed to drink the ship's tap water I gave them. These spoiled darlings only imbibed bottled French Evian water!

Lunch that day was gruesome. The *piece de resistance* (and resisted it was) was a vast slab of not-quite-cooked, watery, boiled ox tongue, in its original shape. Desperate though I was for food, I could struggle through only half of this offering in the interests of survival. The tongue's solitary accompaniment was an unrecognisable green vegetable, which had apparently been boiled for many days. Pam and Mervyn baulked and ate nothing.

Before lunch the captain had caught me in the act of sneaking a squiz at the officers' menu. I had discovered theirs was not the same as ours. The pictures on all the menus were changed daily, and on the officers' menu was always a nude female of some description, on ours a boring old statue. Privilege of rank? I told the captain that this belied their fine French tradition of equality – not to mention liberty and fraternity – and that Pam and I should get a male pinup. The officers then kindly offered to take turns posing for photos to decorate our menu. I am still waiting.

In the late afternoon the sun appeared for a while and, although the ship hit a whacking big pothole every now and then, the sea became calmer. I was told to present myself on the bridge for my lifeboat drill. Crikey! There are no simple lifejackets now. What they have is a lifeguard body suit that you have to get down on the deck and crawl into. You place this contraption flat on the floor and wriggle in, feet first. Then you insert your arms and haul it over your head leaving just a circle of face out. Next you reach behind, pull the zip across the opening, roll that bit around your neck and secure it. All this when in a state of panic! After these exertions you are then expected to waddle like a penguin to the lifeboat. Some hope. This body suit is black and contrives to leave you looking like a seal, which should make you of considerable interest to the sharks. By the time I had manoeuvred myself into that apparatus and got it done up, the ship would have been long since on the bottom of the ocean. But I didn't tell that to the nice young officer instructing me.

Due to the bad weather we were ten hours late docking in Fremantle, Western Australia, the ship's last port of call in Australia. It had been an even wilder night. We had just come through the biggest storm to hit that part of the coast for years. I had been right about Murphy following me onto this ship. At nine in the morning two of the crew came ashore with Pam, Mervyn and I and, courtesy of this, honorary seaman status was conferred on us mere passengers. We were collected at the security gate by the Mission to Seamen's van and taken to the Flying Angel Mission. I had passed this building often when I had worked at the Fremantle Hospital, but never imagined I would get inside it under the guise of a sailor.

I phoned my Perth friends and one came to collect me. We amassed more friends and had lunch at the Blue Duck. This cafe is right on the shore – directly in front of it a couple of years ago, a swimmer was taken by a shark, in full view of a crowd of horrified patrons having breakfast.

I had to be back onboard by five o'clock for the *Manet*'s final custom's clearance before leaving Australia, but it was midnight before we sailed. I went to bed and couldn't sleep until we were moving again.

While awaiting departure I had watched another video with Pam – *Pirates of the Caribbean*, a total load of rubbish. But I hoped the possible pirate attacks I had been warned about would produce buccaneers as good-looking and interesting as those in the film. Johnny Depp would be a good start.

It was another furious night and late the next afternoon we were still below Geraldton on the WA coast. The *Manet* normally can cover twenty to twenty-five nautical miles per hour, but not in the bad weather we were experiencing. The following morning was the roughest yet and I didn't risk a shower. I had already taken one terrific tumble, which had proved to me how simple it would be to break something serious. A sudden wave, bigger and more vicious than those before it, had lifted me up and flung me across the room. En route to the wall I had collected the chair, and the pair of us slammed into the bathroom door, which obligingly flew open allowing us to crash through into the shower. I hit my cheek, arm and thigh and scored a colossal lump, crowned by a magnificent technicolour bruise, on the latter. Regrettably I couldn't exhibit this wonder in polite society. One of the crew had a fall too, which made me feel slightly better.

That day was rather a non-event. I dropped out and slept in the afternoon. The ship was far too unsteady to do much else. In the evening the captain took me to the communications room and set up an email address for me to use while onboard. Unfortunately I had a lot of trouble getting the hang of it, as the French keyboard is different from the English version.

After another violent night we left Australian waters. Then the southern weather was behind us and by Saturday, a week after I had come aboard, at last the weather was calmer. As soon as we were clear of Australian law the bond store was opened. It sold booze and cigarettes, but I was not interested. The wine with meals was enough for me.

I attempted to master the washing machine and must have done something wrong. The instructions were in French and beyond my schoolgirl knowledge of that language and I had to retrieve my clothes wrinkled and wet.

On B deck there was a recreation room that contained a library with plenty of books – many in French – an exercise bike and a rowing machine. I tried both of these latter entertainments, but the bike resisted all efforts to be ridden. What's new? I never could ride a bike.

We had now left the coast of Australia below Carnarvon and were headed out across the Indian Ocean. On my daily inspection of the bridge the sea was flatter, although the sky was still grey, but it was finally warm enough for some of my skin to emerge from its winter hideaway. And in the afternoon we actually saw the sun.

At lunch, which was duck done-to-death in an unhappy way, we were given instructions on security procedures and the crew were ordered to assemble for pirate drill. We were told that from tomorrow, when we neared the coast of Java, we had to lock our cabin and deck doors at all times. Steel bars were secured across the steps that led up to the bridge, one deck down from E deck. We were informed in writing – I guess to cover the ship if we were abducted or killed – that it was absolutely forbidden to go out on deck between six o'clock at night and eight in the morning. Pirates were a very real threat from now on.

Jorg, the jolly Romanian second officer, told me the reason for the captain's stringent precautions. Two trips before this one, the *Manet* had been attacked. In the middle of the night, when only one officer was on the bridge and only navigation lights lit the ship, pirates had sneaked aboard, overpowered the officer, and tied him up. The first engineer had come up to see why the ship seemed to be off course and he was tied up too. Then the first officer approached, but a warning was shouted to him and he ran off to alert the rest of the crew. The invaders were armed to the teeth with machetes and knives and they escaped with everything they could remove from the bridge – lanterns, torches, binoculars, and sextant. Fortunately they did not have guns, or the outcome may have been very different. No wonder we were locked down so severely now.

At four o'clock an announcement, followed by several alarmingly shrill whistles, came over the loudspeakers. As it was in French I figured it wasn't for me, so I did not man the lifeboats. I decided that it was the call for the crew to assemble for the Pirate Parade and, I hoped, lessons in how to repel boarders.

Before dinner there was a cocktail party for the *bo's'n*, a cheerful-looking fellow. It was his birthday and Pam, Mervyn and I gave him a bottle of champagne we had bought from the bond store, and a kiss. Well Pam and I did, Mervyn passed on that pleasure. I managed to remember they do the two-kiss thing in Europe, but found it still wasn't enough. The French, ever greedy in such matters, go in for three. The officers and all the crew assembled in the passengers' sitting room for this festivity while Pam and I sat on the couch like a pair of dowager duchesses and looked them over. We concluded that this ship sported an amazing collection of handsome young men and that they were all agreeable. Apart from the first officer, the cook was the only one we omitted from this category. This lumpy, unattractive specimen leaned against the door of the sitting room blocking our exit. I could imagine him running amok with a cleaver in the time-honoured tradition of eccentric ships' cooks – I'd heard him ranting in the galley, the nasty tyrant. Sadly this was one of the few times I failed in my life's mission to make friends with the cook wherever I go. This one did not want to be my New Best Friend. In fact I don't think he liked me one little bit. Passengers were a trial to him, especially those who wanted proper breakfasts and sent back raw steak.

I managed to elude this terrifying man until one day, as I was sneaking away from my morning's solitary dining experience, I ran right into him. '*Bon jour*,' he said grimly.

I was so rattled I replied, '*Bon soir.*'

Now he would think that I was dimwitted as well as a nuisance. After about a week I saw him again and he smiled at me. Either he thought that it was better to a humour a lunatic, or he had just poisoned my soup.

3 Singapore Fling

From the bridge I watched the ship enter the Sundra Strait, between Java and Sumatra. Sailing at reduced speed through murky, rainy weather, in the company of local fishing boats and other freighters, we threaded our way among the many islands that dot the strait. Here and there oilrigs guard the shore and in the background, Krakatoa's volcano rears its head.

Once through the straight we were in the Java Sea and there wasn't much to look at, so I left the bridge and went below. We were not allowed out on deck at any time now, even during the day. We were in lockdown, like in prison. You'd think this was Pentridge! I couldn't play with the rowing machine, and the gym and library were locked against pirate invasion. I played with the internet instead. But after a while I skulked away quietly from the communications room, thinking that I might have broken the darn thing, and settled myself on my bed with a book.

At seven o'clock that evening the pilot came aboard from the launch that came out to meet us and I returned to the bridge to watch our entrance to Singapore. Having been there a dozen times before, I had not imagined that I could get excited about visiting the city, but now I was looking forward to going ashore. Not counting the day off for good behaviour we enjoyed in Fremantle, we had been at sea for ten days.

To eliminate glare and make the instrument dials easier to see, the bridge was in darkness and it was spooky creeping around it in the gloom. All was quiet, except for the pilot's voice calling out the navigation numbers. I felt as though unseen hands were guiding this massive ship through the dark. In pouring rain we wended our way through a multitude of other vessels, big and small, to the container wharf named Finger Pier. Two sturdy tugs bustled up to push, shove and slot us in among dozens of freighters at the dock.

The lights of Singapore city and the ships surrounding us in the port were very pretty and enticing, but it was too late for anything but bed. With my earplugs in to remove the sounds of the loading and unloading that began almost immediately, I slept.

In the morning there was no customs clearance to negotiate. Singapore is a free port. We three passengers left the ship early. The shore bus took us to the security gate, a long, long drive through kilometres of containers and ships; some of them were absolutely gigantic – Singapore is one of the busiest ports in the world. Then it started to rain again, the first of many tropical downpours at intervals during the day.

I wanted to buy something to make my computer notebook store my photos, so I went to a big, much advertised computer shop. Here an assistant spent quite a long time playing with my machine until finally announcing that it needed a new programme. This would be two hundred dollars. As he also wanted one hundred dollars for a disc I knew cost twenty dollars in Australia, I opted out of this tourist trap. Not on your Nelly, I yelped.

I took a taxi to Chinatown and proceeded to the Peoples' Park complex where, after a lot of footwork, I was told their computer shop had moved. I took another taxi to another computer outlet and, after exhausting more shoe leather, found two polite young men who spent ages trying to fix my problem. Their final solution was that I needed a compact disc player and attachment. This also entailed two hundred dollars, as well as a bulky machine to cart around with me.

I gave up and went to buy a camera battery. In passing, I mentioned my problem to the young fellow assisting me. He promptly produced a tiny card, inserted it into an orifice in the side of the notebook that had been until then undiscovered by me, and the dear little machine immediately said, Oh yes, here I am with your pictures! I could have kissed him. It cost eighteen dollars.

I sashayed back to Chinatown for lunch in a small cafe. Proper food at last! I wolfed down rice, tofu, chicken and an unidentifiable blob of meat covered with lots of chilli.

Feeling now in need of restoration, I had a forty-minute foot massage. In the course of finding this place I passed a house of ill repute. The lurid red lanterns hanging outside it were its calling card. And in the very dark doorway, open to give a view of the even darker interior, two pretty, heavily painted and decorated girls reclined in inviting poses. They, however, did not invite me. Later when I told Jorg, the jolly third officer, about this place, he said, 'Thanks a lot. It will be six months before I am back here. Now if the pirates come I will send them to your cabin.' Was that a threat or a promise? I still had visions of Johnny Depp.

My foot massaging was conducted in a narrow room and it was a communal effort. Six recliner chairs were lined up close together and the male operator sat at my feet on a stool. It's not easy to get a man to fall at your feet in these liberated days, so I enjoyed the experience. The massage was very good, but painful, reminding me I had sworn off foot massages after the last one I'd had in Vietnam. Once again I came out limping, if on air, but refreshed somewhat in the foot department.

I resumed shopping, and at five o'clock, took a taxi to the wharf gate where I sat on a wall to wait for the shore bus to take me to the ship. After a while one of the policemen I had been talking to at the gate drove up in the prowl car and offered me a lift. He said it was dangerous to be out there, loose. I was back to being a loose woman again! Worn out after my exciting day, I tottered up the gangplank and collapsed on my bunk.

At dinner that night I met two new passengers, Rene and Edithe, a French couple, who had joined the ship in Singapore. Rene was utterly dishy. The answer to a maiden's prayer, he was tall, dark and handsome. But as usual there was a fly in the ointment. He had one major fault – a woman in tow. I plotted to push her overboard but unfortunately she turned out to be rather nice. Curses. Perhaps just a gentle Mickey Finn? With my luck, he'd get it.

Rene sported us all French champagne. He had brought 120 bottles of his private wine stock aboard. A jolly time was had by all, and I reeled to bed.

At midnight the *Manet* sailed from Singapore into the dreaded straits of Malacca, reputedly the worst place on earth for pirates. But for us it was an uneventful passage. I spent the next day recovering quietly from the excesses of life ashore on sailor's leave. We passed many freighters and a big white cruise ship, the *Virgo Sun*. That was the only sun we saw, the weather remaining dull. At night there was a stupendous thunderstorm off to the west in the Indian Ocean. The lightning showed clearly against the dark sky that enveloped us and, combined with a line of ships' lights on the horizon, made the sea look like it was lit up for Christmas.

The next day we were through the Straits and, passing the tip of Sumatra, we cast off into the Indian Ocean across the bottom of the Bay of Bengal toward Sri Lanka. I watched from my porthole as a big rainstorm swept the decks clean. It continued to rain almost all that day. But I made out a few ships, mostly oil tankers coming from the Arabian Gulf.

Invited to the officers' mess for champagne aperitifs before lunch, I noticed a pack of Tarot cards on the table. One of the crew told me, 'That's for the captain's weather predictions.'

'Hopefully it's not for directions,' Pam quipped.

That night we put our clocks back an hour and consequently I woke at half-past four, got up at six, and was finished for the day by nine in the morning. Now that the pirate peril was over – we were too far from any shore that offered them hiding places – the ship was unlocked and we could venture out on deck. I had read in the Singapore *Straits Times* that a freighter had been attacked a few days before off the coast of Indonesia. Pirates had fired on the ship but the captain had managed to outrun them.

Finally able to walk on deck, Pam and I ambled around it twice. The *Manet* is 200 metres long and twice around it was almost a kilometre, which was quite enough for one day's effort. The only deck you could walk on was the one below the containers, which was about three metres above the water line. At this level I was low enough to feel like I was walking on water. A couple of the containers were leaking something that smelled suspiciously like fish sauce – a pungent fright awaited the buyer at the other end. The rain had stopped and the crew was out too, painting and doing maintenance jobs. It was terrifically windy – my earrings were almost blown out of their holes when I climbed up to the front lookout, but I did manage to complete my constitutional.

The next morning was sunny and the sea much calmer, with no white caps at all. I spent some time looking out over the ocean's grey-blue, wavy bosom, marvelling at its emptiness. Then, at last, I was able to throw off all my winter woollies once and for all and put on a sarong. The tropics had arrived.

In the library I discovered Graham Greene's *Our Man in Havana*. It was a delight; reminding me of the paranoid CIA man I'd had the misfortune to come to the notice of while working for the US navy many years ago. They had been extremely distrustful of me because I had come to Italy via Russia. Now I ask you! Little me?

We were still losing an hour a day and the clocks went

back automatically at midnight. This day was 31 August and the second engineer gave a party. He said that it was just because it was 31 August, but I suspected that it was his birthday and he didn't want to be kissed. The party was the usual excuse for a knees-up, but who was complaining. This day the cook smiled at me again. My hopes rose. Maybe I had begun to win the battle to enchant him. Or did he just have wind?

4 Damietta Detour

On the third day out of Singapore we passed the southern tip of Sri Lanka and later, leaving the coast of India behind, headed out across the Arabian Sea. Now the weather became calm and the ship moved gently on a mild swell of sea. We were making our way toward the Arabian Peninsula and the Gulf of Aden. During the day I saw two destroyers, an aircraft carrier, and a wooden dhow, sails billowing.

Talking to the crew I learned this was the captain's first command and the first time he had sailed this route. No wonder he needed the tarot cards. The passenger-unfriendly first officer had travelled this track twenty-five times and bragged that he had never been ashore. It showed. Of all the crew, the first officer was the one who looked to be badly in need of some shore leave, as well as some exercise and a good woman. Or maybe a bad one.

Then it was Sunday, our special privilege day again. We had aperitifs with the captain and sat with the officers at lunch. This day kidneys, tough as all get out on a bed of plain rice, was considered lunch. I was the only passenger who ate this unappealing mess. And all of it too. I didn't like it, but I was starving, having missed second breakfast and elevenses.

Sunday was also clean serviette day. Each person had their own serviette and a little linen pillowcase for it to live in. At the end of the week, on Sundays, a pencil appeared on the table and we wrote our names on the pillowcase. My serviette was a quagmire after a week, so it was a good thing it was hidden from public view in its overcoat.

Dinner was a bucket-load of tuna, dry as dust, and a boiled-to-bits vegetable of unknown etiology. The entrée was a couple of fried eggs sitting, dejected and friendless with no trimmings for company, on a big white plate. Rene, who had been a restaurateur until his retirement, was horrified with the food and made frequent jokes about it. It was fortunate that there was a never-ending supply of liquor in which to seek solace. The beer in the store was long gone and there could be no more until Italy, but Rene and Mervyn had laid up secret supplies in anticipation of this calamity.

For the next two days we ploughed across the Arabian Sea. Then, as we approached the waters off the Arabian Peninsula, pirate alert began again. We were no longer allowed out on deck after dark and the ship was under lockdown. On the bridge map Jorg showed me that we were currently off a Yemeni island that some joker had labelled 'Pirate Training Centre'. Between this island and the Yemeni coast lies the stretch of water that, along with the Straits of Malacca, is most frequented by today's pirates – just as it has been for centuries.

Here the swell increased, the sea became disorderly again, and once more wild winds sent spray raining down on the decks. What do passengers do all day on a ship in the middle of the ocean with no diversions for almost two weeks? They investigate each other's history. This would be a dumb idea if you didn't fancy the other confinees, but thankfully we all got on famously. Edithe was extremely elegant, always wore black or white clothes and walked with the incredibly straight back of the ex-dancer that she was. Pam and I shared a like mind as to books. Mervyn was, as he described himself, gnome-like, and a real dear. We were all afflicted with the same warped sense of humour.

Our French friends spoke limited English but we managed. Rene, showing me a photo of Edithe and him at the reception desk of the posh hotel where they had stayed in Tahiti, said, 'Zee 'ow we are smiling? Zat is before zey give us ze bill!'

Edithe told me that her sister lived in Broome, Western Australia. I asked what she did there and she answered what I took to be, 'nurzing'. We proceeded on to a long and increasingly confused conversation about what the hospital was like, etc, until finally we ground to an impasse. Then I discovered that what her sister really did was, 'Nuzzing, 'er 'usband 'as lots of money.' Bully for her. In retaliation for my embarrassment at this misunderstanding, I taught Rene – in exchange for his teaching me to say *allez vous en* – to say, 'piss off', telling him that it was a friendly way to say goodbye. I tempered this by saying that its use should be restricted to customs officers and policemen. That'll learn them I thought.

On Wednesday we finished traversing the Gulf of Aden and entered the Bab al-Mandab, the entrance to the Red Sea. Here the sea became calm again. As we went through the Bab, a speedboat approached us and, waving and shouting, indicated that they wanted to sell us some fish. Their offer was not accepted due to it being fishy.

At this point I could see land on both sides. Africa – Djibouti – on one; the Arabian Peninsula – Yemen – on the other. The Yemen side was closer. There I saw a wide, sandy beach fringed with scrubby growth, rising up to some height. On the highest point a lighthouse stood guard over a few square stone buildings, some of which appeared to be in ruins. The African side showed only an outline of humps and bumps rising from the sea.

The ship was now down to half-speed and as there was little breeze, it became very hot. I grew excited at the thought of stepping onto dry land when we reached Egypt; we had been at sea for twelve days. Now I know what the ancient mariners meant when they said that they 'smelled land'. Even before there had been any land in sight, over the water had come a distinct scent of it, an aroma that reminded me of seaweed and sand.

Having turned the corner around the Arabian peninsular, we were now in the Red Sea. The way became wider and land was no longer visible. The night was balmy, but we couldn't go outside in case pirates made off with us.

As we entered Saudi Arabian waters, the ship's passengers and crew had to declare all liquor and surrender it to the bond store, to be placed under seal before we arrived at Jeddah. I was nervous about Jeddah, even though no one from the ship would be permitted ashore. (The captain found that he was not permitted even to step down onto the wharf to check the plimsoll line.) Would the officials recognise my name on the manifesto? I had been blacklisted in Saudi Arabia for writing about the time I had spent working there! Would they come to take me away? I had a lot to answer for in that country. My fears were probably unfounded but I know how illogical the system in Saudi can be. They could even refuse the ship clearance.

I told Pam that I was going to say I was she and she was I.

'What about the fact that I am sharing my cabin with Mervyn,' she retorted.

'Shacked up with someone else's husband! Yes,' the Saudis would say, 'that's just what she was like. A thoroughly bad lot!'

I woke at four in the morning, when the ship stopped to take on the pilot for Jeddah. As we proceeded on slowly to eventually dock at six, I lay awake. Soon after I heard voices in the companionway and realised the bond store was being checked and sealed by Saudi officials. Their first priority. I froze in case they came for me. All morning I languished in my locked cabin after bolting down for a quick breakfast. Nothing keeps me from my food, not even the threat of arrest and prison.

From my porthole I watched the activity on the wharf. Jeddah's enormous port bustled with trucks and cranes even though it was Friday, the holy day. The call to prayer drifted over the air and wafted in to me. Listening to it took me back more than ten years to my time spent in Saudi Arabia. I relived the terror of the night that I had been arrested. And grieved again for the two hapless Turkish men who had been imprisoned because they let me and two other female workers sit in their empty cafe while we waited for our driver to return from prayers. Explanations had been useless. It had been like trying to talk to someone from another planet.

I felt a great relief when the ship pulled away that evening.

On Saturday I had been on the *Manet* for three weeks. This day we left the Red Sea and entered the Gulf of Suez. On one side was the Sinai, which I could see clearly was desert, but after that I saw no land until late afternoon. Then a hazy outline appeared, beige and grey rises and peaks, all wavy like a drawing done with an uncertain hand. Next came oilrigs – the odd one with an attendant flame. Shipping traffic increased and barren, sandy land with an occasional square building became visible on both sides of the channel.

That night we dropped anchor off the coast of Egypt to await our turn to enter the Suez Canal. We were still swinging at anchor on Sunday morning when, hooray, it was clean tablecloth as well as serviette day. By now our cloth could have been boiled up to make soup.

Out on deck I found the weather warm and sunny. Our ship was surrounded by many vessels, mostly container ships that lay to, waiting with us to pass through the canal to the Mediterranean. On the shore I could see numerous oil installations and big, ugly utilitarian blocks of buildings. This town was Tewfik, where I had spent a happy few days rejoicing in my escape from Saudi. I remembered the pleasure I had taken in the sight of the myriad of ship lights that I had been able to see from my hotel room. I had come to Tewfik from Jeddah by pilgrim ship – sadly the one that sank recently with the loss of over 1000 lives – and had hoped to go through the Suez on another ship. But this plan had failed and I saw the canal only from its banks. Now finally I was to going to sail it.

At eight o'clock the pilot came aboard and we began moving slowly toward the canal entrance. The pilot was a dapper Egyptian gentleman dressed entirely in immaculate white – long pants, shirt, shoes and socks. In contrast, our captain looked like a good-natured, overgrown schoolboy. In his baggy shorts and sandals and with his shirt tail flapping in the breeze, he appeared to be wearing his big brother's clothes.

Commencing our transit, we sailed into the narrow channel of calm, greenish water that was the canal, creeping along at eight knots in a convoy of ships a mile apart. One side of the canal was barren desert; the other, after we passed several no-frills buildings and a large and beautiful mosque at the entrance, was dotted with square, three-storeyed, flat-roofed houses surrounded by gardens of date palms and green vegetable patches. Now and then there was another, smaller mosque or a checkpoint with soldiers bearing guns. This continued for hour after hour. I found a shaded spot on the deck and sat in a chair with my feet on the rail, watching it all slide by.

Even though it was Sunday again, the captain did not grace us with his presence at lunch. He was busy doing the driving. We came to the enormous bridge that spans the canal, and over which the road to Jordan and Israel runs. There was a town on either side of the bridge; both sides had mosques with minarets and ugly, modern, flat-topped boxes of houses. Further on a long row of trucks waited their turn to cross the canal on the vehicular ferries that chugged from side to side, adroitly dodging between the line of ships. Other double-decker ferries took crowds of passengers across, or up and down, the canal. In between all this action fishermen hauled their nets into rowing boats.

After this patch of excitement the desert side returned to expanses of sand, dotted with the odd soldier in a watchtower and now and then tents belonging to maintenance workers or sentries. Toward the end of the canal both banks became empty stretches of sand, followed by long, long breakwaters that we passed between to emerge into the Mediterranean Sea. The transit of the canal had taken eight hours.

Putting on full speed the *Manet* turned left along the coast of Egypt, making for Damietta, our next port of call. We arrived some time during the night and in the morning were still waiting, standing off Damietta, to enter the port. It doesn't bother me to do nothing at sea when the ship is moving, but hanging about, swinging at anchor, became tedious. We passengers were itching to go ashore. Finally, at half-past three, we began to inch slowly toward the line of dots on the skyline that was the town. We passed another freighter on its way out that I presumed was the ship whose berth we had been waiting to fill. Previously I had asked the captain what the hold up was and he said, 'I am waiting for ze bus.'

Strange, I thought, maybe he means a water taxi. Then he repeated, 'Ze bus for ze zip.'

I finally worked out that he was saying *berth*. Sailor-speak for position.

On the bridge I listened to the pilot calling the readings from memory and once again marvelled at the ease with which this great lump of unwieldy metal was inserted so neatly, with two chunky little tugs lending shoulders and muscles, into a spot between two other ships that was only just big enough. Trucks bearing containers moved alongside as we berthed and work began immediately. Time is money in the freight business.

Soon after, the captain said that we could go ashore. The ship's agent would be back in thirty minutes with our passports and shore passes. All tarted up for our long-awaited night on the town, handbags stuffed with money to fritter away in the *souk*, we sat in the lounge anticipating the big event. An hour passed. Dinnertime passed. A bottle of champagne was produced and consumed. Then I was delegated to go down to the dining room to cadge a bottle of red, our rightful due each meal. On the way back I crashed into the officer's mess, waving the bottle, to ask where the agent was. Someone went to phone him.

We drank the wine and became more resigned to our fate as the effects of it hit our empty stomachs. Pam – notice how these not-so-brave warrior wimps sent the women out to do battle with the chef – was dispatched to find food in the kitchen. She returned with bread and cheese. By now the night was quite dark, so all hopes of seeing the town, except by torchlight, had vanished. We decided the inside of a nice restaurant would do just as well. At nine o'clock the next deputation from the women's side, Edithe, went to raid the galley pantry. All caution had now flown to the wind after a second bottle of wine and a few beers. She returned with fruit, a Camembert cheese and more bread. At ten we were past caring and couldn't have made it down the gangplank anyway without sustaining serious injury. And goodness knows what sort of a mess we would have come back in. We decided, huffily, that now we had no wish to see Damietta.

We amused ourselves by sealing a message in one of the collection of empty bottles we had amassed. A call for help. About this time the captain came to see us. I have dim recollections of waving a bottle at him and behaving raucously. He promised us something as consolation. I have no idea what. I strongly suspect I was a mite untidy by bedtime (I was told later there are pictures to prove it). I may have suffered some after-effects; the next morning just before going down to breakfast, I discovered my jeans were on inside out. And for days after our Night of Not Going to Damietta the captain burst out laughing every time he saw me. It's moments like these, I reflected, that you found out who your friends are.

Oh well. So that was Damietta. We were now away for Malta.

5 Landfall La Spezia

Damietta had a lot to answer for. Now we would have only a couple of hours in Malta instead of the day we had been promised. Two mornings after the non-event of our shore leave we held the ceremony of the 'tossing of the bottle' – sending the bottle with its message into the sea and off on its voyage of discovery. We were then in line with the Greek island of Crete and at the widest point the ship would reach in the Mediterranean. The tides could take my bottle to Greece, Libya, Italy, Egypt, Turkey and more. I am still waiting for an answer. Perhaps I should have enclosed a photo. Or not!

That night the ship's engines stopped around midnight and when I got out of bed in the morning we were alongside at Marsaxlokk, Malta's container port. Unfortunately this was too far from Valletta, the capital, or any of Malta's wonderful historic sites, for us to go there and back in the time we had.

We still rushed to go ashore. A bus ferried us to the wharf precinct gate and then we set off walking along the shoreline. Lined with bars and cafes, it looked a much-touristed place. We reached a long cornice lined by gardens, with seats facing the sea against a backdrop of beige-coloured, tightly-packed, square or rectangular buildings. I veered off up a side street to do my own thing. Much as I loved my fellow passengers, I wanted to explore alone.

The town ascended sharply uphill from the seafront, a mass of narrow streets crowded right to their edges by two- or three-storeyed apartment houses. The buildings jostled shoulder to shoulder and there were no yards or spaces between or in front of them. Now and then I came to a tiny shop. In one I bought peppermints and in another, a postcard and stamp. I asked the friendly woman who served me where I could post the card and she said she would do it for me. Everyone was incredibly polite and spoke English in an old-fashioned way, a legacy of Malta's many years as a British colony. I thought it a most likable place, as though I had landed by mistake in a nineteenth-century English village.

We had to be back on the ship in two hours, so I sat down at a seafront cafe, had a coffee and talked to some locals.

As the ship sailed away from Malta we had a good view of the promontory on which the port is built. Lined with ancient caves and small stone buildings, it stretches out to a narrow tip that is crowned with a tall lighthouse. An hour later we sailed past Valletta; all I saw was a row of tallish buildings against the deep blue of the wide Grand Bay that is so famous. I was disappointed not to have had time to go there. Malta will have to wait for another day. Along with Damietta!

We were out in the Mediterranean Sea again. The next day the coast of Sicily slid by. It was lovely out on deck in the cool weather. The Mediterranean was flat and calm and the dark-blue of an Australian sapphire. We had returned to our usual pursuits in the lounge. I looked up from the crossword I had found in the Maltese paper to see Edithe and Rene bent in fierce concentration over a jigsaw and Mervyn and Pam reading. Suddenly I realised we looked like contestants on the television show *Big Brother*; a group of strangers thrown together to sink or swim, to get on as well as we could with no escape. It was a good thing we did get on well together. How could someone be evicted from a ship? Into a lifeboat, or maybe straight into the sea?

Italy and my disembarkation were coming up. The next day we were due in La Spezia, a port near Genoa on the north coast. I was leaving, but the others were going on to England and France. When the bond store opened that evening I bought some farewell bottles. Rum for the officers' mess and an unruly-sounding spirit the captain told me the crew liked, as well as a couple of chablis with which to farewell my fellow passengers.

I was on the bridge when the pilot came aboard. He shook my hand and gave me a hearty '*Buona sera*'. I was back in Italy!

I was not being cleared to leave the ship until the next morning, but I could have shore leave with the others, so I got ready for a night on the town. We sat in the lounge waiting, with our party faces on.

'This feels like déjà vu,' I said.

And that was what it turned out to be. We sat and sat, taking turns to go and ask where the elusive shore passes were. I cracked the first bottle of chablis. We were still there at seven, so, deciding that I wasn't prepared to starve, I went to the dining room for a quick meal.

At eight o'clock the others were given their passes, but mine still had not appeared. I told them to go. They went. I moped about, feeling like Cinderella whose sisters had gone off to the ball, then went to bed in a huff.

The next morning the captain phoned me at eight and told me the ship was leaving earlier than expected and I should get ready to depart immediately. I said goodbye to the crew and suddenly realised the others were still ashore partying on. Thinking the ship would sail in the afternoon, they had said that they intended to spend the night in a hotel. The crew made frantic calls to their mobile phones, but I had to abandon ship without knowing if they had been marooned in Italy. And regrettably, I didn't see them to say goodbye.

I was taken ashore by the ship's agent and left at the security gate where a taxi loitered. Its driver took me for the proverbial ride – thirty-two dollars for an eight-dollar trip. But he did find me a hotel for one hundred dollars a night – which is what they call a cheap in Italy these days.

The Pensione Alberga was a mere two rooms wide, with a dark, minuscule foyer crammed with a mammoth bar. But it was family-run and the owners were kind and helpful. My room wasn't ready, so I dumped my bags and went out walking to fill in time, homeless and in the rain. It was a Saturday in September, exactly four weeks since I had sailed from Adelaide on the *Manet*.

I walked and walked. Parts of La Spezia are very old and the narrow, cobbled streets of the centre where only pedestrians – no vehicles – are permitted have a medieval feel about them. Away from the inner part of the town most streets allow only one-way traffic and other districts are forbidden to taxis or commercial vehicles. Some lovely sites have been preserved, including grand municipal buildings and the governor's palace. Down by the sea an attractive, well-paved and treed promenade runs along the shoreline, while a ring of mountains rise behind the town – their high, green-clad sides sprinkled with soft-coloured villas.

The city centre was also a place where people lived, in tall, multi-level apartment houses fronting the footpaths. Every floor of the buildings sported a balcony, many decorated by lines of washing. There were no backyards for a Hills hoist.

I found the Tourist Bureau, and told the staff I wanted to take another ship from La Spezia to Sardinia, and from there, a ferry to Naples. They said I should try the travel office in the train station. Two buses later I got there for free, as I didn't know how to buy a ticket. I thought the man who got off the first bus with me to point the way to the right bus (I was, not surprisingly, on the wrong bus) was just a kind conductor. Later, when I read my guidebook, I discovered that he was the dreaded ticket inspector, who could have given me a one hundred dollar on-the-spot fine for not having a ticket.

No excuses were accepted for ignorance, said the book. There's a lot to be said for looking confused and helpless.

The second bus I rode knowingly ticket-less. The driver did not sell them as I had imagined he would. These objects came from a mysterious source that I had not fathomed as yet.

I was amazed at what people managed to get onto buses – huge suitcases and bales of goods. Cars were not the norm. Buses ran frequently and the service seemed to be well used. Even dogs were allowed on. If your dog is in need of a restorative after a hard year of hassling the postman and you want to take it on a holiday, go to Italy. Dogs were everywhere; every conveyance I rode had its dog.

After my adventures on buses, I walked for a very long time and to my amazement found that, as if in the bush, I had wandered in a circle all the way back to the town centre and the hotel that was holding my bag hostage.

My hotel room wasn't as big as my cabin on the *Manet*, but it was adequate for my needs. The bathroom was a teeny slit, narrower than a corridor, and lined along one side of it was a basin, a bidet and a miniature shower that was directly opposite an open, unscreened window, through which I could see a man in the apartment across the way drinking coffee.

The three-metre space between our two buildings was an alley, hopefully with no access from the street. The maid had left the door of the balcony and the window undone, so I presumed it was safe. Unless, of course, her boyfriend was a cat burglar.

I rested in the afternoon and after two hours set off again, determined to find the shipping offices; which I did, after receiving many directions. First I tried the maritime museum, which is right on the foreshore and quite something, then I followed the shore along to the ferryboat landings where, in a ticket-sales kiosk, I found a charming girl who pointed me to a nearby office that sold tickets for boats to Sardinia. A notice on its closed door informed me that it had shut up shop on 1 September. Boats did not run after that time, the note informed, as the sea was too dangerous. I was ten days late. Curses! Murphy had tailed me off the ship.

I moved on to plan B. I would stay in La Spezia for three days, then head down to Naples by train. I had not been in this part of Italy before and had read there are some remarkable places to visit up the coast. And, indeed, I was bowled over by La Spezia. It is one of the most beautiful places I have seen.

The Gulf of La Spezia, which cradles the town in a gentle amphitheatre, lies in an area of the province of Liguria that borders Tuscany. For centuries this district has been known as the Gulf Of Poets, its splendour attracting romantics and artists of various persuasions. Ancient Roman poets, eighteenth-century English writers and modern novelists, all have gravitated here to live and work.

After a while I trudged back toward the hotel amongst the throngs of people who crammed the narrow streets, out doing their Saturday evening *passeggiata* (promenade). Saturday must also be wedding day. I passed several people who carried ribboned presents in their hands and saw two wedding cavalcades, horns blaring, roaring through the crowds.

Down by the waterfront I was held up at a street crossing by a religious parade, the blessing of the fleet or something similar. Led by a brass band of luscious, young, white-clad naval officers, a bevy of sailors marched along with a big wooden statue on their shoulders. Behind them trooped flocks of *carabinieri*, policewomen wearing gendarme's hats, and lots of bedecked and gowned priests, monks and nuns.

Once away from the vehicle-free streets of the centre, road crossing was a perilous undertaking. Even main roads didn't have pedestrian lights. You had to risk your life on white zebra lines in heavy traffic. Amazingly most cars did stop. I waited nervously until I saw a white-haired old man with a walking stick step out bravely into the fracas, and shamelessly used him as a buffer.

That night I staggered to bed with a couple of aspirin, absolutely shot, my stiff muscles complaining about the unaccustomed assault on them after a month of little exercise.

I slept late the next day – it did not get light early here. Breakfast was set out in the dining room downstairs. Another deadly continental job, everything was neatly packaged so there was no waste; bread in a packet, and biscuits, croissants, jam and juice in individual servings. But the coffee made up for the bread and jam insult. It was killer coffee.

Once the rain cleared the weather was perfect, just warm enough for pleasant strolling in the quiet Sunday city streets. Church bells rang and people ambled their dogs past me as I stood waiting for a bus. A policewoman, a slip of a girl, rode by on an official police bicycle, her gun in a white holster on her hip. Several people wandered up to join me at the bus stop, all chatting gregariously to each other.

I was gratified by the courtesy shown to me. Taken for a local, countless people addressed me in Italian and were surprised when they realised I wasn't one of them. Sometimes they would ask where I was working. I was pleased I did not stand out as an alien. Decades ago in Naples I had thought that, with my dark hair and eyes, I would blend in, but I didn't. The strange thing was that I was always taken to be German – and, in fact, half my bloodline *is* German. Finally I had made it to Italian status, but sadly, I was no longer addressed as *signorina*. Now I was *signora*. What a difference thirty years makes.

My command of the Italian language began to resurface. It was rusty, but still there after many years of non-use. Having learned it in the market places of Naples, it was not remarkable that the first words I began to recall were the ones for numbers.

A bus took me to the train station where, in an unfortunately functional building, I bought a ticket to Portofino. I was off to see the spectacularly beautiful Riviera de Liguria, the coast north of La Spezia. Portofino is the furthermost village of this area and I planned to start there and work my way back through the other coastal villages by the many ferryboats that link them. Tourists usually take day trips by ferry to the villages, but I had decided to go one way by train and come back by boat.

The railway station was large and honeycombed by catacombs of subways that led to the platforms. The trains mostly ran on time. On the map the train line along the coast appeared a scenic route, but in reality a great deal of it went via tunnels cut through the mountains. The entire coast is incredibly picturesque, consisting of mountains that run down to the sea and villages containing Roman and medieval ruins perched halfway up precipitous hillsides, or nestled into bays between the folds and headlands of the coast. How they were built is a wonder, especially the lone villas that sit high among the dense green of towering mountainsides. I could see no roads, and tracks for vehicles were few. Most of the mountainsides were marked only by erosion lines that rivulets of water had made on their way down to the sea. Travel looked to be much easier by boat.

The train stopped often and took an hour and a half to get to Santa Margherita, from where, for one euro, I took a bus to Portofino. I was getting the hang of using the euro (isn't that a small kangaroo?) for the first time. It was worth one dollar sixty Australian.

Portofino, formerly an ancient fishing village, struck it lucky some years ago and became a happy haven for the rich and famous. In its bay, the celebrated undersea statue, Christ of the Deep, stands on the ocean floor. Why would anyone want to build something underwater? You can see it only when looking down from a boat.

Leaving the bus stop I strolled down Portofino's narrow, cobbled street that leads sharply to the sea. It was lined with minute, but gorgeous, shops sporting names such as Gucci and Armani and offering wonderful goods, exquisitely displayed. Houses and small hotels crowded closely along the waterfront, where scores of boats and terribly expensive-looking yachts bobbed at anchor. One yacht, *Miss Moneypenny*, was decorated by two super-suave young men who lounged becomingly on her deck. I was suitably impressed, as I guessed I was meant to be.

From Portofino I caught a ferryboat to Rapallo, another spectacular village that hugs a small bay further south. At Rapallo I found the boats were not running on this day as the wind had become too strong out at sea. I walked a short way, found the train station and bought a ticket to Monterosso instead.

Monterosso is the first of the five *Cinque Terre* (five lands) fishing villages hidden in deep coastal inlets, or clinging to rocks overhanging the sea, in an area of exceptional loveliness. A train pulled in with the legend *Cinque Terre* blazoned on its side. Understandably, I presumed this was its destination, so I hopped on. I had travelled about halfway to Monterosso when the train stopped. While I sat there, hopeful that it would continue, a female guard sauntered by and asked me if I wanted to go to Genoa. Apparently the train had changed its mind and was now going back the other way. 'Not today,' I said, and scrambled off.

I had to wait an hour for another train, a local affair, very slow and rather seedy, but at least I didn't have to listen to a couple of ghastly tourists telling the world, whether we wanted to hear it or not, their life stories, as I had in the first train. Eventually I arrived in Monterosso and took the ferryboat back to La Spezia.

The boat called in to each of the five villages on the way: Corniglia sits atop a precipitous cliff with eagle-eye views along the coast; Vernazza has steep, narrow alleyways that descend to a natural harbour in a spectacular bay; and Manarola and Riomaggiore, similarly stunning, are linked by the *via Dell'amore* (Street of Love), a wonderful walkway cut into rocks along the shore.

The sea was extremely rough, and the ferry was small, but by the time I reached La Spezia, I had seen almost the entire coastline.

Back in La Spezia I found that no cafes were open on Sundays, but I was directed to a restaurant. As I sat down at one of the outdoor tables under an awning, the waiter lit the mozzie coils that were placed strategically around the dining area. Almost all the tables of the restaurants and cafes were outside on the pavements of the streets and piazzas. I wondered what they did in the winter, as there seemed to be little or no room for tables inside. I ate a divine, two-inch-thick fillet steak filled with Gorgonzola cheese. The first decent meat I'd had in over four weeks – for a devout carnivore this had been a trial. The steak was accompanied by a basket filled with many different kinds of bread, which were also sublime. In my excitement I managed to disgrace myself, first by trying to pour oil on the bread, but sploshing it all over the table instead; then, as an encore, I knocked my water carafe over the lot.

Finally I staggered home, assaulted all the way down the street by very loud rock and roll music. Unfortunately it came from the building opposite my room. Earplugs in, I went to bed and slept.

In the morning I did battle once more with the shower's horrible nylon curtain – a devilish device that took every opportunity to cling lovingly to me. Fending off its advances in a microscopic alcove was no mean feat first thing before breakfast.

This day I had decided to go by boat to Portovenere (old

port), an ancient fortress town that sits, guarding the La Spezia Gulf, high on a headland a few kilometres away. I just missed the ferry. It was throwing off the hawser as I arrived, so I toddled away to find a bus. A smiling bus inspector directed me to the source of all bus tickets, a tobacconist. Aha, I was legal at last.

The marvellous bus ride followed the road along the coast, past masses of naval grounds and war ships. The road was so narrow, the bus filled it entirely and had to toot madly as we approached corners, and back-up when we encountered another vehicle.

I thought Portovenere was fascinating. Built as a completely walled fortification, it had been well established, according to Roman records, in AD 160. At that time this area had been an important maritime and naval centre, and it remains so today. The oldest part of Portovenere is still a walled village, which is entered via a rounded stone gateway. Once through this I proceeded to labour up a very narrow, almost vertical, cobbled street lined by small, tightly-packed houses. The house doors opened directly off the cobbled street and on a mat in front of one, a big ginger cat sat patiently awaiting entry.

The front rooms of some of the dwellings contained tiny jewels of shops with bay windows displaying goods for sale: food, souvenirs and jewellery. Small shops in Italy tend to sell only one line of goods – bread, wine, or cheese for example, all of which I found to be superb in Italy. I had noticed a shop near my hotel in La Spezia that sold only items of soap, all decorated with large price tags.

On my way up the lane, I saw the sea lapping at the outside walls of the lower houses and now and then as I passed open doorways, I caught a glimpse of a set of steps leading down to the water where, tied at the bottom, a small boat gently rocked. It reminded me of Venice.

I huffed and puffed to the top of the village and there, on

the highest point, was a magnificent castle, the Andréa Doria. An example of Genoese military architecture, its imposing walls loomed over the village.

Later I went down to the ferryboat landing to return to La Spezia, but once again I missed the boat. A plague of loud tourists stood in front of me asking interminable questions of the patient ticket seller. They queried every little detail – you'd have thought they were going to buy the ruddy boat – then tried to pay with a credit card. In this, a tiny canvas kiosk on a dock! By the time they left, so had my boat. I went cursing past the African vendor on the footpath. I saw many of these people selling goods by roadsides and guessed they were refugees.

So it was back to the bus for me. I found the only place to buy tickets here was from a machine. I failed this test and asked the bus conductor to do it for me. It is good for the soul to make somebody feel superior.

In La Spezia the bus stopped in a street near my hotel where a big market was in progress. It was held in the piazza under an attractive metal roof built in waves like the Sydney Opera House. There were flowers, food, fruit, jewellery, clothes and junk. I can never resist markets. The ambience in this one was excellent and I had a leisurely wander around. I passed a *carne di cavallo*, a horse-meat shop, and shuddered. Although I will happily scoff any other animal, somehow the thought of eating such a beautiful creature as a horse repels me.

At the food stalls, all I needed to do was look and point to buy bread, olives, cheese, grapes and nectarines, all of which were very good. Then I sat in the park and had a picnic.

Italy was no longer the extremely cheap place I remembered it to be. Market produce was about the same price as it is at home, but eating out was dearer. I quickly learned that if I stood up at a bar to have my *demitasse* of espresso coffee, as the locals did, it halved the price. Even wine was expensive.

What had happened to the litre bottles I used to buy for sixteen cents? I saw water for sale everywhere at around forty cents per litre, so I presumed it was still not safe to drink the offerings from the tap. Petrol was almost two dollars a litre. And getting by when travelling alone on one hundred dollars a day would mean living starvation style. Single room prices were nearly or the same as double rooms.

Early next morning I took a taxi to the railway station and bought a train ticket to Naples. Then came the fun part – getting my bag up and down endless flights of stairs and negotiating through labyrinthal, subterranean depths to the right platform. But the wait on the platform was okay. It was a cool, clear morning.

Trains stop only for a short time in stations, so I had to get onboard fast. The conductor threw me and my bag into the first available open door. From there I wobbled and weaved through seven swaying carriages to reach my seat, on the way meeting several dogs and a fat tabby who glared at me from his basket in the corridor.

6 Napoli Nostalgia

From La Spezia the train travelled at first among mountains encrusted with rose-pink, beige and ochre-coloured houses and pocketed by many tunnels. Later there were vineyards and cultivation between towns that all looked the same. An occasional castle on a hill gave interest to the scene. I was seated in a six-berth compartment with an assortment of people who all offered me a share of their food. We passed through Pisa, but no tower was in sight, and after six hours arrived at Napoli.

At Stazione Centrale, Napoli's central train station in Piazza Garibaldi, I asked the woman at the information booth to recommend a local hotel. I knew this district had an unsavoury reputation. Not only is it a haunt of villainous street people, criminals and members of the *Camorra* – Napoli's home-grown version of the Mafia – but also many of its hotels moonlight as brothels. However it was a convenient location for me, a good base for what I wanted to do.

I was given the name of a nearby hotel that was said to be respectable and close enough to walk to. And I did. I was improving. Making my way to a new hotel on foot, wheeling my huge bag, was something I had thought I would never be able to accomplish.

The hotelier was a grumpy old man. I think he was having a row with his wife; there was a lot of shouting going on. But then again Neapolitans shout a lot at any time, so I couldn't be sure. The room I was given on the second floor was an agreeable surprise. It was old but spacious, and had an attached bathroom, two balconies and all mod cons.

Cleaned up, I went out on a reconnaissance mission. Napoli had been my home for two years way back in the 1970s when I had worked as a nurse in the American Naval Hospital at the NATO base. At first I had shared an apartment in Via Manzoni in Vomero with three other Australian nurses, and then I'd found a tiny flat on the beach at Licola Mare. And I had almost married an Italian man of considerable charm. I had promised to return to Italy and now I was here I intended to revisit my former haunts and look up my old fiancé.

Right now though, nostalgia gave way to hunger and I sat down to eat a pizza in the train station. I couldn't come to Napoli, home of the original pizza, and not do that. Somehow it tasted different here. Everything you could ever want can be found in that railway station. Although guidebooks tell women to give the area a miss at night, it was safe enough in the daytime if you were wary. The petty crime rate is high everywhere in Napoli, but the station was well supplied, especially at peak time, with a large amount of police. Big Alsatian dogs accompanied some, while others rode about in little Fred Flintstone buggies that looked like children's toys, despite the official blue lights atop them.

I came across a travel agency where an obliging man told me how to get to Arco Felice the following day. According to the phone book my friend still lived there. While in the phone booth I tried to contact Rome to check on my onward passage. Forget it! Public phones take your money and refuse to give it back if the number is engaged, which it invariably is. Returning to the agent, I asked him to phone for me. The news was bad. No cabin vacancy existed on a ship heading south down Africa way. So it was on to plan B again. I booked a flight.

Before leaving home I had investigated the best and cheapest way to get to Madagascar if no ship became available. It was to fly with Air Mauritius, via Mauritius, from where there was also a direct flight to Perth, which would be ideal for my return home.

I went back to my hotel room for siesta. It was in a major street that ran past the train station, well away from the insulated tourist part of town. Earplugs counteracted the noise of the traffic. When I stepped onto my balcony that hung over the busy street, I could look down on the cafe underneath, see all the way to the railway station, and feel part of Napoli. Strangely, one of the room's balconies was attached to the bathroom. This room had been remodelled and I use that term loosely, as that's how it had been done. Long and wide, it was the extreme opposite of the one I'd had in La Spezia. It had a huge shower and a marble floor, but horribly dim lights. After fixing my face and hair in front of its mirror, who knows what I went out looking like.

Early the next morning I set off to do battle with Napoli's public transport. The Grumpy Old Man hotelier cheered up when I told him I would remain in his hotel for the six nights of my stay in Napoli and we negotiated a price. Thirty-six small kangaroos – fifty-six dollars per night. Southern Italy was cheaper than the north.

I breakfasted on coffee and a pastry standing at the bar in the station, then headed for the trains. Napoli has an extensive local underground train system called the Metropolitana that also connects to the funicular. The dead opposite of the underground, the funicular cable car scales mountainsides in nasty, panic-inducing little boxes.

I began my odyssey on the Pozzuoli train line, along with crowds of students heading for the university with art folders tucked under their arms. The young people were all dark, slim and attractive and dressed in the latest fashions. When I had lived in Napoli previously I had been warned that respectable girls did not travel alone on public transport. I did it once and lived to regret it. I was pinched black and blue. Had women acquired more equality since those days? Or was it just my extreme age that protected me now? Not a pinch in sight! No one tried to accost me in the street either. I couldn't decide whether to be depressed or happy.

The names of the stations were familiar, but as most of the line travelled underground, I didn't see much of the city. At Pozzuoli the station cleaner courteously told me that I was on the wrong line – I should take a bus if I wanted to reach Arco Felice.

The bus stop was nearby, among the impressive Roman ruins and arches of Pozzuoli, beside an attractive park. The bus took an hour to materialise, but, sitting on a wall swinging a leg, contemplating 2000-year-old Roman arches, was a fine occupation for a sunny morning – which eventually became afternoon by the time the bus came along.

In Italy train and bus tickets are interchangeable. They cost one euro and last for ninety minutes. If you don't leave the system you could, theoretically, ride forever. Or you can buy a three-euro ticket that lasts all day, which was a good investment in my case as I spent all day getting to one destination. And what a difference being a tourist made. Because I'd had Italian connections when I had lived here, I had rarely done the tourist bit. I'd had my own transport too, a well-used Fiat 600 that I had bought on arrival. So, never having ridden on a bus along this route before, and given the amount of change that had occurred in my absence, I rode through the Arco Felice area without recognising where I should get off. I went on, past Bai with its wonderful castle standing high on the hill, then Bacoli along the Bay of Napoli with its brilliant views of the sea and ships, before finally coming to rest at Monteprocida, the terminus.

By this time I had the bus to myself and after a chat with the driver and a share of his fruit, it was decided that I should ride the bus back to Napoli with him, as it didn't return through Arco Felice. We picked up a jolly, if deafeningly noisy, bunch of teenagers coming home from school and approached the city centre along the downtown part of the Bay of Napoli where flotillas of ships waited to leave for Sicily, Capri and Ischia.

The bus finished its journey in Piazza Garibaldi, off which many small back streets crowded with market stalls meander. I made my way to the hotel for siesta through these thoroughfares, chomping on a huge baguette stuffed with ham and salad.

After suitable restoration, toward evening I sallied forth again on the train system. Getting off at Mergellina, I walked down streets lined with cafes and restaurants, where patrons sat at roadside tables, to reach the funicular that is winched up a steep hillside to the heights of the Vomero residential area. But instead of providing vistas of the city lights as I had hoped, the cable car travelled almost the entire way in a tunnel. I left the funicular at its terminus on Via Manzoni – and there was the view, exactly as I remembered it. Wonderful. From high above the city I gazed down on the entire Bay of Naples – surely the most beautiful bay in the world – and across it to where Mount Vesuvius stood sentinel over it. The lights glittering around the bay, on Vesuvius and on the ferries crisscrossing the dark water, were just as they had been when I last saw them. It was good to be back – to find this once-loved panorama unchanged was a real joy.

More small shops lined Via Manzoni now and it appeared more commercialised, but the row of tall apartment blocks where I had lived remained the same. I found a greengrocery with colourful fruits spilling out onto the street, and bought some grapes. They were three times the price of those directly below at the entrance to the funicular. The price must increase with altitude.

I sat to eat my grapes in a small park where people came to admire the view. From these exalted heights even the ghastly downtown traffic snarls took on a fairy-like air in the night darkness, the taillights of vehicles in one-way streets twinkling red and white. I was joined by a couple of mums who had brought their toddlers to the park to play with a ball. Apartment living provides no backyards for kids to play in. The same applied to dogs and evidence of their visits decorated the street.

The next day I resumed my adventures with the rail system and discovered that I could reach Arco Felice by train. Not that I did on my first attempt. I went past the stop. You have to know where you are, and I rarely do. I took another train back and, after a toddle in the sunshine, there it was – the site of my pilgrimage, my former fiancé's home. It was changed, but recognisable. I asked the maid for him by name and was told that the *padrone* had died the year before. It took me a while to realise that he had become the *padrone*, the family head. I had left it too late.

I declined the offer to meet the family. I had been drawn back to Napoli by unfinished business. I had come to Italy to lay my ghosts. Now it was done.

In a daze I decided to continue on to Licola Mare to see if my old apartment was still there. My map showed a train line that went to Licola on the map, but didn't tell me that I needed to change trains. The map went to Licola Mare, but the train didn't. I spent ages waiting at bus and train stops. That writer who said it is easy to get about on Napoli public transport is right – as long as you have infinite patience, all the time in the world, a fair knowledge of Italian, and view maps with cynicism.

Four trains and two buses later and I was back at my hotel at six, having been a lot of places, but not the one I wanted – Licola Mare. The driver of the last bus had been a young, slim and trim, beautiful blonde girl who easily could have made the cover of *Vogue*. And she drove like a champion. One hand nonchalantly resting on the window ledge, she wove her ponderous vehicle in and out of horrendous traffic tangles and belted at breakneck speed through the many tunnels of Napoli. People still drove anywhere they chose in this town. It was impossible to tell which way a street ran, as vehicles would be all over it going both ways, or preferably, down the middle. I read that the traffic was supposed to be better now. Than what, I'd like to know. It seemed about the same to me – madness itself.

There was still little in the way of rules – no seat belts or helmets and drivers parked anywhere, at any angle and on any side of the street. A parking inspector would have been in heaven, his pencil worn down to a stub! But even here, to my astonishment, traffic on the streets would mostly stop for me. It was a game of nerves. You dared them to have a go at you, and with any luck they missed. But from the frequent sound of ambulances, I guessed they didn't always. No matter how dense the traffic was the locals would walk into it. I learned that what I really had to watch out for were motorbikes, which would appear, like avenging angels, out of nowhere and scream past, scaring the life out of me. In Napoli I sank to the depths of using children as air bags to get across roads.

The next day I set off for Licola Mare by train. There was some way of identifying the trains, but this was only available to the initiated. As Flip Wilson said when dressed in drag: 'What you see ain't necessarily what you gonna get.' However, after three days experience I had the drop on the system; there was only one change of train and no mistakes.

The station was a long walk from the main street, but it was a lovely day. A car came creeping past and I received the first, and as it turned out, the only offer I got this time in Italy. I refuse to describe the man making the offer on the grounds that it would damage my image, not to mention my pride. I had plummeted low on the attraction scale from my early days in Napoli. Then I couldn't stand still on a street or walk anywhere without cars trying to entice me in. Mind you, that was how prostitutes operated then and all the men seemed to be in a perpetual state of longing. That I had looked as though I was available for this activity had annoyed me no end. Once, when I had my hand in a big bandage and my arm in a sling, one man would not leave me alone. A hospital freak? I got so mad I put my sturdy Italian boot, bought from the *mercato di scarpe* (shoe black market) into the side of his sleek silver Ferrari. A Ferrari no less! You'd have thought he would have had more finesse.

At Licola Mare I found my old apartment block easily. It was down a lane, right on the sand of the beach. I'd had the minute rooftop penthouse four floors up. Very little had changed. The village still consisted mainly of one long road with houses and apartment blocks strung along it.

I waited for the bus that ran down the road. It returned to Pozzuoli via an inland route, not beside the water's edge on the road that I had rattled along to work every day in my tinny little Fiat.

7 Arrivederci Roma

Another daily train ticket and I was off again, this time to Vesuvius. Somehow, despite living near it for so long, I had never managed to visit this famous active volcano. On the train an enterprising chap serenaded the passengers with a piano accordion, angling for a tip. I gave him some money hoping he would go away. He wasn't to know that piano accordions give me the willies. Unfortunately, it inspired him to even greater endeavours, so I had to grin and bear it.

Many stops down the Vesuvius line I came to Castellamare where I changed to another funicular, this time a cable car that is pulled up the side of the volcano in the open air. Into this shaky little horror I stepped with trembling knees. Only after it had wobbled off did I remember the awful story I had been told when first I had come to live in Napoli. A few years before that, the funicular cable had snapped and eleven people had hung, thousands of feet up in the air, suspended between life and death by a few threads. For hours the Italians had run about crying *mama mia* until the last strands severed and the passengers plunged to their deaths.

Three people and a dog joined me in the cable car. Everyone except the dog and I enjoyed it. I was stupefied with fear as I saw the ground dropping from under my feet. The dog whined pathetically and grovelled on the floor. I wanted to join him. I felt safer when we rose higher and were above the thick, dark-green forest that clothes the entire top of Vesuvius. The bottom of the car seemed to be brushing the treetops. Then I felt as though I knew how the birds felt and my fear subsided slightly.

I put my tremulous self out at the top of the cable car track, only to find I had no option but to go back down in it again when it was time to go. What did I do on reaching the top of Vesuvius? Head straight for the loo of course. Then to the bar.

Vesuvius is certainly awe-inspiring and, as it is an active volcano, is probably due to erupt again. That was what happened to Pompeii. But up there on top of the world I forgot all that. It was so cool and, despite the restaurant and cafe that flank the cable car exit, so peaceful and quiet.

I hiked through the forest to where I could look out over the countryside all the way to Napoli. I cautiously trod the path, a dirt track presumably made by mountain goats, which was scary in places, but I had it all to myself. Unlike the summer months when tourists tramped about, at this time of the year no one else was in sight. I was wrapped in the tranquil beauty of the place. There were pine needles underfoot, and pretty mauve flowers that sprang directly from the soil without leaves, like autumn crocuses. The fresh air was marvellous.

But I still had to face the descent. Somehow it was better knowing that dear Mother Earth was getting closer and not further away. And the view was great.

Blasé now about catching local trains, I made my way back to Piazza Garibaldi and on to Piazza Cavour, the town centre where the tourist action is. The guidebook mentioned churches that shouldn't be missed – with not a word about the fact that churches shut up shop for siesta. The first church was enmeshed in an 'it could only happen in Italy' type drama. A crazy man paced the highest of its steps, ranting to the folk who had assembled below to watch the show. Three police cars and an ambulance stood by. I figured the performance had something to do with his wife leaving him.

The ambulance attendants, having finished whatever they had been doing, stripped off their rubber gloves and threw them on the ground. This was normal. Litter abounded in the streets and there were few bins. The council rubbish cart trundled around daily, but Napoli managed to defeat it. It remained much grubbier than northern Italy. The top of Vesuvius had been layered with litter and not a bin in sight. Railway stations were the same.

I found Napoli's *duomo* (cathedral) in a street that looked wide on the map, but in reality was a tiny space of rough cobbles where the houses almost met overhead. Some streets were barely the width of one vehicle, so narrow I couldn't imagine trying to drive through them, but cars still managed to negotiate their way along, pedestrians flattening themselves against the wall as they approached. It was a good thing most cars were small here.

The cathedral is huge and spectacular and contains much fine Carrara marble. Everywhere I looked in this part of Napoli, in narrow streets or grand piazzas, I saw churches and magnificent buildings. But I wondered at the cost of all that splendour in a country as poor as Italy has been at times. As I sat on the cathedral's marble steps waiting for siesta to finish, a good-looking girl with a child in a pusher approached me. It took me a while to realise that she was begging. She looked me squarely in the eye to make her appeal. I gave.

The inside of the cathedral was glorious, from its painted and decorated ceiling down. The Feast of San Gennaro, in celebration of the patron saint of Napoli, San Gennaro, was due in two days time and nuns were busy arranging flowers in large brass vases. The crypt containing the saint's tomb lies under the altar, at the bottom of a flight of dimly-lit marble steps. Finding it rather creepy, I didn't stay down there for long. The precious relic of Saint Gennaro is a vial of his blood, said to have been saved at the time of his martyrdom. On his feast day the vial is taken out and examined and if it liquefies, all is well, if not, a disaster is forthcoming. I wished I could be here in two days time to see what happened. That was the day I was booked to fly to Madagascar. It would have been handy to know if there was about to be a major catastrophe.

The next day, Sunday, I explored the markets in the back streets around Piazza Garibaldi. Although this is the area most advised against going to in the guidebooks, I was happiest there. Its tiny narrow alleys with their uneven cobbles and ancient arched portals teem with life. Everything imaginable is sold here – new, old, stolen, black market. I bought a pair of designer sunglasses that were so hot they sizzled when I put them on. There were pretty, glittering bead necklaces and a mountainous barrow-load of silk scarves at half a euro each. I bought two. One had a tiny mirror embroidered onto the back of it. Was that so a mugger could titivate himself up to look good while coshing you?

Trash and treasure abounded. On one junk stall I spotted a large and beautiful old Japanese imari bowl for three euros. It broke my heart to leave it there, but I knew I couldn't have brought it home alive.

Napoli is famous for its seafood and all kinds were on offer: mounds of shiny black mussels; knots of live, black eels writhing, long, skinny and sinuous, in shallow pans; and silver fish in baskets on the cobblestones.

Snack food was for sale on stalls and in bars, and eating out seemed a universal pursuit. Stalls overflowed into the lanes and alleys and spilled out to clutter the footpaths of the piazza. There were many black African vendors, but I noticed they didn't sell in the alleys, only in the piazza.

I was not the only one out for a Sunday ramble – the lanes were packed with shoppers and strollers. This was no place for anyone unhappy in crowds. And noisy ones at that. But the people seemed good natured and tolerant of each other.

I noticed though that almost everyone smoked – especially young women – and in the street too!

After siesta in the evening I walked again. This was my last night in Italy, hopefully not for another thirty years though. I ate next door to my hotel at Cafe Scugnizzi. *Scugnizzi* are the homeless street kids of Napoli and former street kids run the cafe. When I had lived in Napoli I had met the priest who did a lot of work with them, Father Mario Borrelli – the subject of Morris West's book, *Children of the Sun* – and had been enlisted into his brigade of volunteers. Photos of street kids as they had been before rehabilitation lined the cafe walls. Its kitchen prepared meals for paying customers, while food for the homeless simmered in large cauldrons.

This night I was served the very best gnocchi I have ever eaten. I had no idea this dish could taste that good – the sauce was to die for. The cafe service was not so hot, but the tablecloths were a cheerful red and it was pleasant to sit outdoors at a sidewalk table, separated from the passers-by by a low rail and some pot plants, sipping a vino in the warm night air.

The next day was the big one: I was off to Madagascar! Wheeling my bag to the train station was a breeze, for it was getting progressively lighter as I cast away my winter clothes, though I was not sure that even the poor would be glad of something that I had finished with.

A good thing about Italy is that their atrociously expensive taxis – I read that it cost eighty dollars to take one to the airport from the train station in Rome – were compensated for by cheap public transport. But if I hadn't learned from past errors about the necessity of asking three people the same question to arrive at an approximate answer, I would never have caught the train to Rome successfully. The station's information board gave the train's number, but not the platform. The train, however, was not marked with the number that was on the board, and the destination in front of it on the platform was Milan not Rome. Still, it was a super train and the nice travel agent who sold me my ticket had booked me one of the single, spacious seats at the end of the carriage.

It took this express train less than two hours to reach Rome. Soon after it pulled out of the station I heard snoring coming from the seat in front of me, and I too relaxed. In Rome I had only one flight of stairs to contend with and a man carried my bag down them for me. Someone usually offered to help me if I looked pathetic enough. Then it was a smooth drag to the train that goes straight to the airport's interior. I found a seat in a compartment right by the entrance door and next to the toilet.

I am like QE2 who, sensible woman, is said never to miss the chance to use the loo. I couldn't find anything in there that looked like a flush though, except one big red button. I pushed it. It was the emergency alarm. A very loud siren set up a hideous clamour. I sneaked out and slunk to my seat, but a red light was on in there too and the bell was deafening. Two men went to get it stopped. To no avail. For the entire half hour it took to reach the airport the alarm shrieked hysterically. I wondered how good the system was. If this had been an emergency it had been ignored.

Rome airport is immense. There are long, long stretches of motorized walkways, which are a blessing, leading to A, B and C terminals. I travelled kilometres and paid visits to them all, as well as Arrivals and the shopping mall, before coming to rest at the right check-in.

During the long wait for departure I ate some very expensive food and then positioned myself where I could watch planes coming and going. Security was tight. There were many checks and I saw some men of Middle Eastern appearance stopped, questioned and searched.

Finally, an hour late, I boarded the Air Mauritius plane. It was terrific. One of the latest models, it had personal video screens and food that made Qantas meals look like the offerings from a soup kitchen. They served bucket-loads of French wine and lashings of French-inspired food. I got a bit blurry and so did the film I tried to watch – an old one with Humphrey Bogart and Peter Ustinov. The pilot's voice matched Ustinov's – unlike the announcements in Rome airport, which had been incomprehensible. And the flight attendant broadcasted in an accent that I'd previously only heard in the Queen's Christmas message.

I was nervous about flying all night over all the water of the Indian Ocean but I slept, thanks to the vino, for an hour. Then daylight dawned and it looked as if we might make it, so, after a good breakfast, I cheered up.

In Mauritius the flight to Madagascar was delayed for over an hour. Slumped in the airport waiting room, the only white person under the scrutiny of a room full of local people, I felt seedy and looked worse. I was no advertisement for my race. I put my head down on my bag and tried to blot it all out in sleep.

Finally on the plane, a great lunch restored me and forty minutes later we touched down in Madagascar, 250 kilometres off the East African coast in the Indian Ocean, the world's fourth largest island.

8 Madagascar Achieved!

In Ivato, the airport for Antananarivo, Madagascar's capital, I collected my bag and was besieged by a mob of would-be porters and taxi drivers. At the change counter I discovered that a new currency, the ariary – 15,000 to one Australian dollar – was now in play and it seemed to have improved the exchange rate. Everything cost less than the prices quoted in my guidebook. This was an admirable twist; it is usually the other way around. The woman at the money exchange counter told me how much I should pay for a taxi to the town, I found a driver who agreed to this price, but reneged when we got there. A bargaining session followed, after which I had to pay extra to get rid of him.

It took forty-five uncomfortable minutes in a rattle-trap Renault to cover the fourteen kilometres to Antananarivo. My first look at Madagascar was singularly uninspiring. We careered along a narrow, winding road, passing traffic – mainly tinny old Renaults and Citroëns – that came at us full pelt, swerving all over a road that had no marked lines and, apparently, no rules except Rafferty's. The buildings that bordered the road seemed about to fall down. Mostly wooden shanties with boards crooked or missing and bits tacked on them in odd places, they jostled against each other all higgledy-piggledy, interspersed by countless tiny ramshackle stalls and shops.

Occasionally I saw a better house, a skinny two-storeyed edifice of red brick built in a style I had not seen before. They had high peaked roofs like chalets, with dormer windows in the peak and first-floor balconies supported by thin wooden columns. But even they were not intact. Most had chunks gouged out of their walls or other glaring faults. Everything was dry and dusty. I thought it a desolate-looking dump.

The people we passed, for the most part, were dressed in unpretentious style – men in trousers, and women in long skirts or sarongs with long-sleeved blouses.

Tana, as the local people call their capital, not surprisingly, given its proper mouthful of a name, is situated on a plateau in the centre of the elongated island of Madagascar which measures roughly 1600 by 570 kilometres. High on a series of hills, and surrounded by rice paddies, Tana has been Madagascar's hub since ancient times, as well as the capital of the former French administration.

Approaching the town, the buildings improved, but the roads stayed narrow and winding. To enter the street that contained the Shanghai, the hotel I had selected from my guidebook, the taxi had to stop at a roadblock and submit to a boot and engine search by gun-toting soldiers, as well as a going-over with a metal detector. Later I learned this street had soldiers, police, guns and barricades at every possible entrance to it. It harboured the American embassy. What a place to pick!

The Shanghai's receptionist, who was never without a smile, spoke English, one of the few people I met in Madagascar who did. She let me have a room for 30,000 ariary – about twenty dollars – but said I could stay only for one night, as the place was full.

Grateful for small mercies, I fell on the bed and slept till teatime, when I surfaced to eat in the attractive downstairs dining room with its bright décor and crimson tablecloths. Another agreeable disclosure was that the food was not only cheap, but also very good. I had read that rice three times a day was likely to be my fare in Madagascar, but here I had

Chinese steak with lots of mixed vegetables. It was the best meal, nutrition wise, I'd had since I had left home. It cost six dollars. Fantastic. Due to years of faulty government and civil unrest, Madagascar is a poor country and prices seem low to travellers.

My room on the second floor was also good value, and the squeaky clean bathroom had a marvellous big bath, deep enough to drown in, that was a soothing shade of aqua. The bed had enough blankets too – I needed three even though it was almost October and summer was approaching. Madagascar's seasons are the same as in Australia, but the climate varies from cool in the mountains, to warm on the coast. The eastern side of the island has tropical rainforests while the western, in the rain shadow of the central plateau, has dry deciduous ones.

A notice on the back of my door laid down the rules in Malagasy and French – both languages are in general use. (It is essential to have a little French to get about on your own.) A garbled English translation accompanied the notice. It began with 'Pleasant clientele', continued with warnings such as 'Take care of you self in fire', and ended with, 'Your comprehension is appreciated, signed The Direction'.

I felt they were hoping for a bit much in the comprehension component. Malagasy goes in for an almost pathological use of letters. The word zoo, for example, is *saha misy bibidia hojerin ny mpitsangantsangana*. I rest my case.

The Shanghai Hotel is near the Haute Ville, the up-market centre of Tana; translated as 'high town', it is just that. To get there the next morning I had to gasp my way up the long flight of cardiac-arrest inducing steps that ascend to it from the end of my street.

At the top of the steps I wandered into what I thought was the post office and stood patiently in a queue until a young man asked me what I wanted. I showed him the letter I had come to post and said 'stamp', or so I thought, in French. He shunted me to another queue where I stood for ages while a woman made a transaction. Finally I discovered that I was in the bank. So much for my French!

The post office was almost next door but I had to run the gauntlet to reach it. Pushers of postcards and handcrafts assailed me on all sides. The PO was a small room with several computers for using the internet. I don't think they did much posting there. The two stamps I bought cost two dollars, a fortune by local wage standards; the average annual income is around three hundred and fifty dollars.

The Malagasy people I had met so far were softly spoken and charmingly tolerant of my ignorance. It was good to be back in a country where the pace of life is slow and relaxed. Traditions of hospitality and kindness to strangers make it a welcoming place for the lone traveller. The family, including distant relatives and ancestors, are the centre of life. Every woman I saw seemed to have a baby adhered to her person somewhere and there were toddlers en masse underfoot in the streets.

Up here in the rarefied air of Haute Ville I saw some decent buildings that were not falling down. This is where the grand live, along with foreign embassies and the town's most prestigious hotel, the Colbert, a relic of the French colonial days. Legions of guards with rifles hung about these streets.

At checkout time of twelve o'clock I was ejected from my admirable room into the street and rendered homeless once more. But the kind hotel receptionist phoned nearby places of residence until she found one willing to accept me – the Residence Anjary. I walked the couple of streets it took to get there. The footpaths of most streets were very narrow, as well as broken, with cars parked over their edges and across them, leaving little space for pedestrians to walk between them and the walls of buildings.

Coming from the airport, I had taken one look at Madagascar's shabby streets and somewhat down-at-heel people and thought that I would never be game to walk about here, but twenty-four hours later there I was, out on the street, feeling perfectly at ease.

My new room was very big and it had a kitchenette. It was really a bed-sitter unit and, according to the name on its door, it was called, intriguingly, Beryl.

I moved in. Beryl was not without her faults. The entry door was made of transparent glass and opened into a wide passageway, off of which issued the bathroom. In order to reach this haven, half-asleep and in a state of undress in the morning, I had to risk exposing my charms to the passing public. And even with all the lights on, I needed a guide dog to get around after dark. And the noise!! Lawks a mercy, where was the Noise Pollution Patrol? From a petrol station next door, hideous music blared at maximum decibel level straight into my room on the second floor. What would it be like to work down there I wondered. You'd have to be deaf, I presumed.

To escape from the racket I went walking and accidentally discovered the Basse Ville (the lower town), the commercial heart of Tana. It straggles along the two wide streets of Avenue de l'Indépendance, which, separated by a broad median strip, runs from the railway station at one end to a grand flight of steps – they reminded me of the side of a Mexican pyramid – leading up to the Haute Ville at the other. I had thought that I'd escaped from stair climbing when I had left the ship, but in Tana there were steps everywhere. The French, out of necessity due to the district's extremely hilly terrain, had built two gigantic staircases to join the lower and upper parts of the town, as well as one that leads up to the road that ascends to the royal palace on Tana's highest peak.

In the Basse Ville post office I tried, but failed, to use the internet. Had I been able, it would have cost a mere two cents a minute. At a snack bar I balanced on a high wooden stool among a crowd of local people, and, helped by a young male attendant, ordered a marvellous chicken and cheese baguette. Baguettes, omelettes, good coffee and fabulous bread and cheese were French legacies here.

From the two big streets of the Basse Ville, the town climbs sharply up the encompassing hills, with tier after tier of buildings stacked, like blocks, to their very tops. Verandas and arcades that house shops, commercial premises and cafes, shade the buildings along the sides of the two streets. All the shops had guards stationed outside them, and all the guards wielded business-like batons. In this crowded part of the town the pavements were packed with pedestrians, hawkers, beggars and the homeless. The beggars accosted me. One had a face and hands eaten away by leprosy and many were children, unbelievably dirty and ragged, but with appealing little faces. I sprayed money around. I gave to women with babies, and cripples, and to a boy who played a drum and sang on the steps. I noticed that local people also dropped small coins into beseeching hands.

I wondered if anyone ever bought anything in the dusty and almost empty-shelved shops when, outside them on the footpaths, an endless stream of hawkers offered an endless array of goods. Some sellers hounded me to buy the most unlikely items a traveller could want. One boy chased me the length of the street convinced that the article I could not do without was a new wheel for my bike. That would go well in my bag, I thought.

The interiors of the shops were dark and they had aged wooden counters and wooden floors. Everything looked as though all the clocks had stopped one day in the 1940s and time had stood still since. In search of something to read I tried a *librairie*, a bookshop. Staffed by six nuns, it sold only religious literature. The nuns, although graciousness itself, were gently determined that I wasn't going to escape without buying something and they sold me a postcard. Even in a small shop it took two people to serve me. The person with the goods didn't handle the money. For the purchase of a twenty-cent postcard I was given a receipt written in duplicate with carbon paper.

I did find a street vendor selling the local English language newspaper. I had no idea what was going on out there in the world, and after reading every word of this four-page tabloid, I still knew nothing. But it did contain a quote from Confucius that I loved: 'The man who stands on a hill with his mouth open will wait a long time for the roast duck to drop in.' My sentiments exactly!

After siesta with my earplugs in, I walked in the dark to the Sakamanga Hotel, a short distance away, for dinner. Never mind the danger of muggers; the real death traps here were the broken, battered pavements. At night you needed a torch to survive. Some of the holes in the footpaths were so deep you could disappear down them and never surface again. And the streets are cobbled with small, slippery uneven bricks which, even without the added excitement of the occasional mini mineshaft, made walking about an adventure and sensible shoes essential.

The Sakamanga is a popular place. It has great atmosphere and superb food. In Madagascar I found the French cooking and cuisine I had expected on the ship. This night I had fish, a considerable amount, in a smashing sauce accompanied by green beans and something else in the vegetable line that was orange. Fruit followed: a big plate of papaw, pineapple and banana. Total cost, eight dollars.

Returning to my hotel, on the pavement in front of it, I passed two Flowers of the Night, as the gentle Balinese charitably describe them. Dressed in microscopic miniskirts they patrolled up and down, teetering on very high heels. I suspected that the hotel might be their place of business.

The floor below me later hosted a screaming and shouting tournament that went on for most of the night.

I returned to the Sakamanga for breakfast, had a fabulous ham and cheese omelette, two baguettes and a three-cup pot of coffee for four dollars, and set off again on my shanks pony tour of discovery.

Coming across a pharmacy, I checked to see if they had the latest anti-malarial tablets. They were one hundred dollars for twelve. I left them there. There is a new drug, derived from wormwood, a bush that I had seen growing around fowl yards on farms when I was a child. I remember my aunt telling me that it was grown there because it kept parasites off the hens. I suppose this may have been because they ate a little of it now and then. I wondered why the government of a country as badly affected by malaria as Madagascar could not plant a few bushes. This new drug is available in Australia and I would have liked to try it, as it has no serious side effects, but it is prohibitively expensive to take for an extended time. Instead, I was carrying a few Malarone – also hideously expensive – not as a prophylactic, but to treat myself if I got malaria. I believe that if the eradication of malaria in developing countries were taken seriously, something would be done about the price of medication for it. Drug companies make obscenely huge profits.

One debatable modern trend has reached Madagascar. On a board outside the pharmacy I saw a clinic advertisement offering the dubious beauty treatment of 'plastification'! It promised to lift your face, straighten your nose and make you infinitely alluring. Opting to keep my crooked nose and my fallen face, I moved on.

Planning my future movements with the aid of the travel guidebook, I decided where to go from Tana. I had come to Madagascar to undertake a wonderfully varied mix of activities. I wanted to ride the antique train from the mountains to the coast, visit the island that used to be a pirate's haunt and, especially, to see lemurs. The wildlife of Madagascar is unique. Due to its isolation, ancient forms of creatures, long gone from the rest of the world, have survived here. Originally part of Gondwanaland, along with Australia, Madagascar broke free of Africa over 165 million years ago and gradually drifted east to its current position. It is home to some two-thirds of the world's species of chameleons; the ancestral home of the lemur; and the majority of species of plants, insects and mammals found here do not exist naturally anywhere else in the world.

In the past there had been a train from Tana to Toamasina – formerly called Tamatave – the seaport on the east coast, as well as the towns of the centre. The railway was rumoured to be starting services again. Checking this information with travel agents I found in offices around the upper town, three told me there was no train, but the fourth said there was. Because that was what I wanted to hear, I believed her. Foolish, gullible woman that I am, I galloped, light of foot and with girlish hope in my breast, to the railway station at the far end of the town.

'*Oui, oui*,' said the lady station attendant. 'There is a train.' This I could clearly see. It was standing right there in front of me on the rails. But even with my faulty French I could tell that she wasn't going to sell me a ticket. The train went nowhere. It was there only as a decoration.

I left the station not with a train ticket, but a silver moonstone ring bought from an Iranian jewellery exhibition nearby. I justified this madness by telling myself that it didn't take up much room in my luggage, and I continued on to look for a bus.

I was told that there are no buses. Madagascar's tourist industry is still fledgling and mainly attracts small French groups who hire minibuses. Lone travellers are few and getting around is not easy for them. Due to the size of the country and the often difficult terrain, roads are scarce and frequently in poor condition. *Taxi brousse*, bush taxis, are what take the place of buses for local people. I had read of these apparent instruments of the devil and didn't relish the thought of an encounter with one. A bush taxi is a small van into, and on top of which, is crammed and crushed the maximum possible amount of goods and people. And they have a formidable reputation for crashes and breakdowns.

Worn out by the search for transport out of Tana, I tottered back to rest during siesta. The shops, and anything else that possibly could, shut for a two or more hour lunch from eleven o'clock.

A gracious woman at Dodo Travel, an office that I chanced upon by accident in my later evening foray, told me about the bus that four previous tourist agents and two hotel receptionists had denied existed. A real bus, as opposed to a *taxi brousse*, it was a new service called Madabus, but I didn't let that deter me. I had noticed in Madagascar that, in ignorance of its significance in English, many things are called Mad. Would you trust yourself to Mad travel (it sounds rather like what I do), eat in Mad cafe or, a real worry for a white-knuckle flyer, take to the skies with Mad Air, as Air Madagascar is generally known?

I paused to donate to a beggar crippled by bilateral talipes, who sat on the pavement among the passing crowd. Talipes, club foot, is a congenital problem that is no longer seen in first world countries because it has been possible to correct it fairly simply for at least fifty years. I was sad to see that here a young man was condemned to the life of a beggar for the want of medical care.

Tana has two supermarkets. I investigated the one in the Haute Ville. I couldn't find anything light, i.e., without sugar or fat. I supposed this wasn't necessary in a country where many people looked to be in need of all the calories they could get. Local prices were cheap but imported goods were dear. In a glass cabinet, under lock and key, lived that utterly precious item, Nivea hand cream.

That evening I went to the Shanghai for dinner and was told I could move back there the next day when a room would be available again. After a peaceful rest, the morning was cool and overcast. Once more established in the Shanghai's comfort, I breakfasted under the knotted bougainvillea that forms the roof of a pleasant courtyard, then took a taxi to Madabus to buy a ticket.

The taxi took me on an unscheduled tour of the surrounding hillsides, up and down and all around, on sharp, winding and narrow roads, before disgorging me at the hotel where Madabus was reputed to hang out. The hotel denied all knowledge of a bus and sent me next door. They sent me to the corner shop, whose proprietor sent me down the street where I climbed a flight of steps, went through an old wooden door, and in a bare room that contained only a desk and a chair, I finally achieved the purchasing of a bus ticket – to Ambrosita. I had decided to head south to see what the centre of the country was like.

Now for an adventure in banking, Madagascar style. Needing to change some traveller's cheques, I took a taxi to the Hilton Hotel where my guidebook writers – I've got it in for these people – once again lied to me. They said there was an American Express office there. There was not. And the receptionist told me ever so gently that I wasn't considered a suitable person to change money in their establishment. I slunk out, deflated.

I walked all the way back to the town around the edge of Lac Anosy, the large lake beside which Tana is built and which supplies the town with water. A big statue of an angel, a monument erected by the French for the Malagasy who died fighting beside them in the First World War, dominates the centre of the lake. At the lake's edge white egrets stood so still in the calm water that their mirrored reflections presented perfect images and I could have sworn there were two of them. Where part of the lake's bank rose to higher ground, a row of barber shacks squatted along its very rim. Rough, rickety tumbledown wooden huts, they were so tiny two people couldn't get in at once. The victim sat inside on a chair with a shelf and a mirror in front of him and the operator stood outside and worked from there. All the barbers smiled and said '*bon jour*' as I went by.

So far I had learned only one Malagasy word – *salama*, good day or greetings, the same as in Arabic. The rest of the language was beyond me. I tried, but it totally defeated me. Just learning to say goodbye was going to take a time. *Manorapihaona* – try saying it.

I moved on to attempt extracting money from a bank. When I asked the teller if the bank changed traveller's cheques, the reply was, 'Yes, please wait.' I stood at the counter for ten minutes before the manager approached. He denied me any funds and sent me on to the next bank. They said, 'Yes, come back after lunch.'

I tried a third bank, feeling like Goldilocks. Here the cashier smiled and said, simply, 'No.' I asked her where I should try next. She said, 'Please wait', returned after five minutes and started filling out the forms to give me the money. Strangely, the one person who said no actually changed my cheque, though I did get big smiles from all the others.

But it would have been pushing my luck to hope that I could get the hard cash there and then. I was told to come back in two hours to collect my loot. And loot was exactly what it felt like as I was stuffing the wads of notes into my money pouch. By the time I had secreted away 480,000 ariary in small denomination notes, I looked as though twins were on the way, but I waddled out happy.

9 Mountains and Monarchs

I soon learned that the Malagasy, although far too polite and gentle to actually hit you, strenuously object to being called African. Although the country is geographically part of Africa, it is an independent republic, and proud of it. I saw all kinds of faces in the streets, some with the fine features of Ethiopians or other people from the north-east of Africa, and some who looked Indonesian. Now, around half the population follow indigenous beliefs, a bit less than half are Christian and just under ten per cent are Muslim.

Depending on which source you read, Madagascar is thought to have been settled somewhere around 2000 years ago by people from Indonesia/Malaya who came in outrigger canoes via southern India and east Africa. Today the population of around nineteen million is made up of members of eighteen main tribes or clans living in the areas that were the old kingdoms before the country was, largely, unified under the strongest of these, the Merina by around 1808. The Merina kingdom was forged by Andrianampoinimerinandriantsimitoviaminandriampanjaka, and his son, King Radama I, went on to conquer most of the rest of the tribes on the island.

Arab sailors knew of the existence of Madagascar; they called it the Island of the Moon. Marco Polo was the first European to report the large island in the Indian Ocean, and he called it Madagascar. The first Europeans to sight the island, in 1500, were the Portuguese. They called it the Red

Island because of the colour of its soil. Attempts at colonisation by various European countries failed due to disease and resistance by the local people until, in 1817, the British entered diplomatic relations with Radama I. They instigated trade and sent aid and missionaries, who converted the Merina court to Christianity. The next monarch, Queen Ranavalona I, a truly fearsome woman who indulged in some appalling hobbies, such as sawing her enemies in half, threw all the foreigners out, which in view of her disposition, was probably lucky for them.

Later it was the turn of the French, who, in 1896, succeeded in making Madagascar a colony, and it remained so until independence was achieved in 1960, at which time the French retained control of trade and finance but a government committed to revolutionary socialism came to power.

Today Madagascar is a republic with a president, prime minister and a parliament. Unfortunately, from 1960 until 1989 the government's policies of nationalisation of private enterprises and centralisation of the economy crippled the country's finances and caused many French to take their expertise and money out of the country. In 1989 restrictions on criticism of government policies were lifted and general strikes, riots, coups and upheavals followed until, in 2002, civil unrest on a grand scale erupted over the presidential election results. Marc Ravalomanana, a contender in the election and a reformist, swore himself in as president. He received United Nations endorsement and since then all has been relatively quiet.

On Saturday I found that many Tana businesses were closed, while some worked only a half-day and went home at eleven. I laboured up the eighty-five steps to the Haute Ville again. Tana's high altitude still had me staggering by the time I made it to the top, but these steps were mere child's play compared to the ones that led there from the lower part of town. I had started counting steps as I panted up them. It helped to pass the time and relieve the tedium. There were sixty-one up to my room at the Shanghai just for a start. I hadn't counted the bigger flight down to the Basse Ville. The downhill march didn't bother me. There were plenty of distractions along the way – countless hawkers and beggars fringed the wide expanse of the steps.

At the top of the eighty-five steps I donated to a beggar woman and her baby, and in the post office I bought a phone card, which I was told I could use to call overseas from any phone box. I had doubts about this, it sounded far too easy.

Down a narrow street near the post office I came to the plush hotel Colbert and, having heard that it had a pool and spa that were simply the ant's pants, I went in for a sticky beak. The ground floor foyer was adazzle with enormous glinting chandeliers and tremendous marble floors, but sumptuous was the word for the pool. Beneath the foyer, subtly lit, it was other-worldly and subterranean. Aqua mosaic tiles and lush green plants made the glittering water of the pool look green too. This luminous green world was like a scene that had escaped from a Hollywood version of ancient Rome. Romanesque urns and statues lurked discreetly in the gardens and the absence of a utilitarian pool edge added to the feeling that this was a rock pond in a magic cave. The sauna and the change rooms were equally sublime. The staff cheerfully showed me around even though I probably looked far from the usual ilk of guest they were accustomed to in this salubrious establishment. But they did make me take off my shoes.

I taxied up to the Musée d'Andafivaratra, the national museum that stands far above the town, near the palace on the summit of the highest hill. It was a long winding road, but I didn't realise how steep it was until later when I started walking down it. I had to brace my legs and lean backwards to stop from falling flat on my face. But I discovered that I quite like walking downhill, although I did wonder how those poor, grinding, clapped-out taxis – the ridiculous Renaults that resemble Freddo Frogs and the Citroëns that look like matchbox toys – make it to the top.

The taxi dropped me beside a flight of ancient steps that curved up a high rounded wall. At the top of these broken, crumbling stairs I found a substantial old building in very bad repair. In the dusty, uneven forecourt a piece of cloth was strung between two bamboo poles, and from over the top of it a wet female head on a set of bare shoulders examined me. From the sound of splashing water I assumed that I had disturbed a lady taking her bath. Nevertheless she graciously told me that the museum was next door. Or rather she pointed that general direction when I said, '*Musée*'.

I hiked down the steps and followed the high wall around a bend and up more steps, grand this time, and then I saw the museum. It was the former palace of the prime minister, Rainilaiarivony, the enterprising gent who is said to have been the power behind the three queens he married in succession. Set back from a sweeping carriage drive and fronted by a courtyard with several huge trees, it was an imposing, dusky-pink, baroque pile. A guard told me that I couldn't go in, as it was closed because the roof had blown off in the last cyclone and hadn't been fixed yet.

As I ventured in for a closer look, a troupe of nuns appeared walking in crocodile file, one young novice wearing an improbable straw hat over her veil. I waited until they came level, loitering with intent, then, inserting myself among this holy lot, sneaked into the building with them. They obviously had better credentials than I did. In the foyer of the former palace, two big wooden staircases ascended, one on either side, to the upper stories. It appeared to be only the top part of the building that was still awaiting repair. A guard materialised and indicated that I could go into the room on one side of the foyer with the nuns, but that the rest was off limits to me.

In this room I found a comprehensive display of fabrics. In the past the weaving of cloth was an important part of female Malagasy life and wraps and stoles are still worn or given as tokens of regard and high office. All the exhibits were accompanied by detailed explanations in Malagasy, French and, wonders never cease, English. As I was leaving a small gaggle of French tourists arrived with a guide and were allowed into the other downstairs room through the main entrance – the guard unlocked a substantial pair of heavy wooden doors in the foyer for them.

He saw me peeking in and now asked if I was willing to pay 5000 ariary to go in too. Maybe I hadn't looked as though I'd had the money before. Happily I coughed up the required three dollars fifty and was permitted into the inner sanctum.

Wow. It was worth it. The French mob's guide/keeper raced them around and herded them out in a few minutes – then I had it to myself. There's a lot to be said for travelling alone.

I was in the reception room of the palace. It was circular, a couple of football fields wide, and had a fabulous glass-domed skylight in the centre of its lofty ceiling, which made the room light and airy. On the first floor a balcony of carved wood ran around the entire level, with arched doorways leading off to rooms. On the next level up there was no connecting balcony, the doors opened onto their own little balconies like boxes at the theatre. There was no access to the floors above from the reception room; the only way to reach any of the rooms would have been via the staircases in the foyer.

Alone in this great empty place, with no sound except the wind whistling past the glass dome way overhead, I walked slowly around the exhibits. I was glad to see that many of the Merina rulers had been women. Queen Ranavalona I, that dreadful woman with the nasty habits, had owned jewels that fascinated me: heavy, intricately worked earrings, necklaces and bracelets of gold and turquoise; several large crosses set with amber, one of filigreed gold and emeralds which looked real, but one of an improbable blue that I think was correctly labelled 'small glassware'.

Another case contained the coral jewellery only the nobility were permitted to wear (along with anything red-coloured). There were coral necklaces, bracelets, earrings and crosses, again wrought in wonderfully worked designs.

The royals had been big on oil portraits. Queen Ranavalona III's picture showed her as a fine-looking young woman, but the fashion police would have rushed her straight to the slammer. Her treasures included an evening bag that you couldn't give away at trash and treasure and a hat, like an upholstered tea cosy, that I wouldn't be caught dead in. Beside this monstrosity were two of her wigs. I was not surprised that she felt the need for wigs; you'd have to disguise me too to get me to go out in that hat. But I lusted after her lovely toilet set of twenty silver-topped, cut-glass bottles, containers and jars.

Also on display was the fine outfit that was worn during *betaly*, the circumcision rite performed on royal males. The paraphernalia included hefty shields and belts of copper trimmed with gold and heavily encrusted with multicoloured fake, but pretty, stones. All very splendid, but poor compensation I should think for losing a piece of one's anatomy.

It was gratifying also to discover that this royal lot had at least one common human failing. The burial accoutrements included a couple of glass-stoppered bottles still full of what was obviously hooch.

I found a sign that said 'Iron ladies', but as there was no sight of Maggie Thatcher or Imelda Marcos, I presumed it referred to a couple of beat-up old ladles. This was the translator's only mistake, so it was perfectly excusable.

The boots of King Radama I, the first king of the united country, didn't look like they'd done a lot of walking, but the wooden chair on poles for carrying him about on the shoulders of his serfs explained that. I bet he hadn't had to slog up those millions of steps and hills like we mere mortals did. In one glass case there was an enormous ornate bible that had been a present from Queen Victoria and in another, a massive lidded brass ale jug and a set of tankards embossed with an English hunting scene. Pretty useless, I would have said. You'd need a barrel of ale to fill it and two strong men to lift it.

There was a magnificent gold and red velvet throne that had been made in England for King Radama I – it looked a lot like the one our Liz sits on now and then. Then there were the crown jewels, another impressive pile of clobber. The crown was solid gold. It had no jewels but the gold must have weighed a ton.

I decided to walk back to the town centre and, with the brakes on to stop a headlong hurtle, sped down the hill. At various spots I stopped to admire the marvellous view over Tana, and was surprised to come across three tiny shacks, suspended on the very edge of the towering mountainside, that housed shops and eating places. They were planks of wood leaning against each other rather than buildings, and contained a box for a counter and few goods, just a bottle or two. They may have been in the Frightful Slum category of architecture, but anywhere else they would have had amazing real estate value for their position.

Lower down I came to a site where I could hear running water. Looking over the wall that edged the road, I saw a creek that ran sharply down, burbling through bushes, among trees and over black boulders, rocks and ledges. People were washing themselves and their clothes in the stream. These folk appeared to live there, devoid of any shelter except that offered by the vegetation. It made me wonder where the street people of the town slept. These unfortunates were in such a miserable state that it always hurt me to look at them. I wondered how they kept trying to exist from one day to another when it seemed there could be no way out of their predicament.

They seemed to have no future. I guess it was the primal urge to survive at all cost.

Further down the hill the sky began to spit light rain on my head and I sought refuge in a church, a hulking stone structure high above the road. Passing a wedding car parked at the bottom, I puffed up forty-odd stone steps of a six-metre-high fortification. The car, a shiny dark-blue Mercedes, had been decorated within an inch of its life. White bouquets and ribbons fluttered on the bonnet, the boot and all the door handles.

At the top, I gatecrashed the wedding, peering in from the porch with several women holding babies – I suppose they had been ejected due to bad behaviour. The wedding was the full catastrophe white affair. The spacious church was packed with guests decked out in their finest and the light reflecting through the many stained-glass windows fell softly on the happy couple, who knelt before the altar at the far end of the impressive interior.

The rain increased. This was the only day I had gone out without my umbrella – even here in Madagascar Murphy had found me. A handsome young man, also complete with a squalling baby, joined us in the porch. I was pleased to see that female emancipation had arrived here.

The rain finally cleared and so did I. As I went down the steps the congregation burst into song with 'Oh god our help in ages past'. I thought the words of that hymn hardly fitting for a wedding, unless perhaps the groom was nervous about the arrangement.

I followed the wall along the road for a while and came to another set of stone steps that led up to the back of the church. Beside the base of these steps another highly decorated car was parked, a red Citroën with multicoloured bouquets all over it. Why the back door, I wondered? Was this for a fast getaway in case the groom chickened out? Maybe he really was nervous.

Saturday must have been the day for weddings. Every

church I encountered was hosting a wedding party, with decorated cars standing guard outside. As the weddings finished the church bells began ringing with 'Here comes the bride'.

Further and further down the hill I zipped, passing many walls, all of them five or more metres high. Perhaps they were there to hold the buildings on the mountainside. I passed men playing a gambling game by the roadside using small squares that looked like scrabble pieces. Children were everywhere.

Five kilometres later I made it to the bottom of the mountain, and headed to the Salamanca Hotel for lunch. The food was great but the dining room was packed with French tour groups, who smoked up a bushfire all over me while I ate. At least I didn't see the locals, especially women, smoke much. In the markets and streets I saw men buy cigarettes, one at a time, from vendors who had wooden trays containing open cigarette packets slung around their necks.

Outside the restaurant I gave my change to a young woman who sat in the gutter with a baby and two toddlers. Then it was back to my room for some R & R and a little surreptitious washing (for some obscure reason it was illegal to wash clothes in the Shanghai, but I didn't have the time it took to wait for my clothes to be returned from the laundry).

For dinner I ate in the downstairs restaurant and had frog's legs in garlic, messy but delicious. The frogs served here were small and you ate them with your hands. I took chilli with everything I ate, as a prophylactic against stomach complaints – even my breakfast omelette. A local concoction was always on the dining table with the condiments. It contained chilli, garlic and ginger. I defy any bacillus to survive that.

I now had a room on the fourth floor. It had double glass doors leading to a small balcony and through them I looked out, over the rooves and gabled windows of the neighbouring buildings, to the town. The drop underneath the narrow balcony precluded my wanting to venture onto it – I felt sick the only time I tried this, but I could see across town to the hills. Apart from the houses of the rich and the elegant buildings in Haute Ville, much of the town looked in bad repair. Some of it had already collapsed.

In the morning I spent some time in the garden writing on my mini-computer. It had become colder, and Madame, the owner, flitted about the breakfast tables wearing a raincoat and a red woolly scarf.

10 Mad (about) abus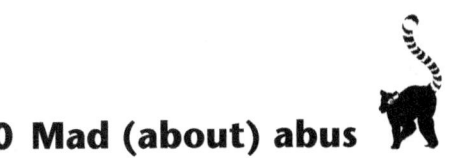

On Sunday morning church bells were tolling as I made my way through the crowded footpaths outside the churches. Those worshipful places certainly got a workout. I was out to explore Tana further, tripping along a narrow road that edged an alarmingly sudden drop down a hillside, with no rail to stop your fall.

In the Basse Ville I was foiled in my efforts to use the phone card I had been promised was simplicity itself. I moved on to investigate the Analakaly Sunday market. It sprawls along the Basse Ville's Avenue de l'Indépendance from the side of the staircase that leads up to Haute Ville. Cat Stevens serenaded me from a nearby CD stall with 'Father and Son' as I bought soap. The seller asked me for 5000 ariary. I countered with two and thought I had done well until he gave me my change. The price had been 1000. I had misheard him. So much for my astute bargaining.

I proceeded back up to the top of the mountain to visit the Rova Palace, the former residence of Merina royalty. Refusing the cigarette the driver politely offered me, I folded myself into his rusty Renault taxi for another assault on the hill. Engine flat out, revving madly, and whenever there was a slight decline, roaring to get up steam, we approached lift off. It sounded as though there was a goblin banging away with a hammer under the bonnet. These taxis seldom had rear door handles – had they been removed to stop passengers escaping without paying?

At the Rova's gate I took on a guide – there were no signs with explanations – a charming young man who, in heavily French-accented English, told me about the palace. Its wooden interior had been destroyed by fire in 1995, but the outer stone structure remained, still a commanding edifice.

Tana's location had been chosen for reasons of security – it was not only high in the mountains, but its sharp slopes would have been very hard to attack. The palace had been built on the highest hilltop of all. A gigantic bronze eagle, presented to Madagascar by the emperor Napoleon, loomed over me as I went through the wide entrance gate. The eagle roosted on a stone phallus on top of one gatepost and another stone phallus stood on top of the opposite one. In keeping with the phallic cult of the country, both were circumcised.

From the parapet wall that surrounded the palace grounds, I looked down on expansive views of the city and beyond to the heart-shaped Lac Anosy. It amazed me that this land could have been built on at all; the drop that fell away under the palace walls was utterly precipitous. Queen Ranavalona I, never one to miss an opportunity for a new method of execution, had instigated the spiteful practice of throwing her enemies off the battlements. (One up on being sawn in half, but still pretty hair-raising.)

Silhouetted against the sky, on a high strip of land on one side of the palace, were two small houses. Rada, my guide, told me that they were tombs; one for kings, the other for queens. Unlike any tombs that I had seen before, they resembled the spirit houses of Asia, but were much larger, more human sized, and came complete with windows. I asked Rada why tombs would need windows. To which he answered, 'Why, to see out, of course,' and gave me a funny look that said, silly tourist, what else? Then I discovered that the interiors of the tombs were equipped with beds, tables, chairs and all the necessities of life. The spirits lived there. Even those Malagasy who profess other religions still hold firm to the ancient animistic beliefs; especially *hasina*, the force that flows from the land, through the ancestors and into the living. Worshippers bring food and drink to the ancestors and they are consulted about important decisions. The most intriguing ancestor ceremony is *famadihana*, the turning of the bones. In August and September tombs all around Madagascar are opened, and corpses taken out, danced around and chatted to. They are then re-wrapped in new burial clothes before being returned to await their next outing.

Rada told me that sacrifices are still made to the ancestors, but now humans are not killed, only animals. That sounded bad enough to me. I've met a few animals I would scratch off the list of candidates for this doubtful honour before certain humans.

A stockade of high pointed palings enclosed a small wooden corral beside the palace. Rada said that this had been 'to keep the cow in', not, I imagined, for milk, but while it was waiting to be offered up in sacrifice next door.

Rada also explained that it is *fady*, taboo, to point at the tombs or to enter some palace doorways with the wrong foot. *Fady* is encountered all over the country and is taken very seriously. It can take the form of the prohibition of a certain action, or a forbidden food.

Inside the palace grounds stands a replica of the original Merina palace. Made entirely of wood, one door is carved into the shape of two breasts, a matriarchal symbol signifying that this was the queen's as well as the king's room. In a corner of the room, on a wooden platform high off the ground, sits the royal bed. Their majesties had to climb eight wooden rungs to reach it. More rungs on the wall next to the bed ascended almost to the top of the extremely high, pointed roof, leading to a platform among the rafters. Here the king was reputed to have taken himself in order to spy on the queen's visitors. I hope he had good knees.

My tour of the Rova finished, I gave Rada a handsome tip and trotted back down to Tana. Rain began sprinkling, but this time I had my brolly with me. I took a shortcut, successfully for once; you can't go wrong when your destination is clearly visible from where you are. Coming to the long flight of almost vertical steps – I counted exactly 250 – that descend from the hillside, I nipped down them to their terminus in Avenue de l'Indépendance. A deep drain ran beside the steps and along it tumbled a trickle of water and the most gruesome mess of rubbish.

Passing the post office, which was shut, I noticed the internet office upstairs was open. I decided to make yet another stab at conquering this devilish device. True to my server's name, at first it was as dead as a dodo. Then, when I was almost ready to give up trying to work out what the French instructions meant, I managed to get through. Amazing!

The internet attendant could not change a 2000 ariary note – all of one dollar forty. I promised to come back later with the money and, such is the trusting and generous nature of the Malagasy, she merely smiled and said, 'Bien'. Afterwards I wondered why I had not just given her the 2000 ariary and not bothered about receiving my change. I guess it's that sometimes you can lose touch with the real world when travelling and forget that 2000 ariary is not much. It just *sounds* like a lot! In order to get some change and return to pay my huge twenty cent debt, I had lunch in a nearby *Salon de Thé*, a teashop. Another French legacy, these *patisseries* offer sumptuous-looking cakes and pastries as well as the usual cafe food.

In the street I was pestered excessively by a couple of beggars. I baulk when I am harassed too much, but I still feel sorry for the harasser. If you are desperate, I suppose it helps to be persistent. However, instead of folding to these two, I gave my small change to an old man who sat quietly with his cap on the ground in front of him. At one stage I found the hand of one of the beggar woman's children, a half-grown boy, in my bag. Just as well I had my purse tied to my knickers by a long string and my passport around my neck. (I felt as though I was dressed in armour to go into battle with the knights of old.)

At dinner in the Shanghai I ate with the young American man who had stopped me in the street that afternoon to ask directions, and discovered he had just arrived in Madagascar to study parasitic diseases in the south of the country. As he was the first native English speaker I had come across since I had left the ship, I talked my head off. When I finally paused for a bite he told me how, the night before in Johannesburg, he had been robbed of three thousand dollars. I offered help to tide him over but he said he was okay.

I slept with one eye on the clock and got up at half-past-four. I had to catch the bus to Ambositra at six. The hotel's watchman who, poor man, had to spend the night in a wooden hutch by the gate, organised a taxi for me. When I set off at half-past-five it was only just light, but the streets were already coming alive. Street sweepers plied old-fashioned witch's brooms past the homeless souls curled up asleep on the pavements.

I hurried along, worried about missing a seat, but I was the first to arrive at the spot where Madabus waited in the street. Eventually a young French couple joined me, and just after six another two rolled up. We took off thirty minutes late with a total complement of five people rattling around in this twenty-four-person bus. Ten minutes later we stopped for petrol – it was one dollar fifty a litre. A few minutes after that we stopped again. This time the driver and his co-pilot stepped off with pieces of paper with 'Madabus' handwritten on them and fixed them to the windows with sticky tape. I wondered why until we came to the first of many roadblocks. The police waved us through, but they pulled over bush taxis and frisked the passengers. Were tourists above suspicion or had Madabus come to a financial arrangement with the *polizia*?

It was still early, but crowds of people strode along the roads to work. At seven in the morning! Later schoolchildren appeared – some in navy skirts or shorts and white shirts, while others wore grey with pale-blue lab-type coats on top.

Fifteen minutes later and we stopped again, this time for the driver's breakfast. Mind, he did ask us if it was okay first. I was hopeful of sustenance too, but the stopping place contained only a row of deplorable shanties labelled *Hotely*. This, I had learned, denotes a small down-market eating house and not a hotel. I was the only traveller intrepid enough to risk the coffee. The *hotely*'s chipped and battered enamel mugs were being washed in a tin basin on the ground in water from goodness-knows-where but, ever prepared like a good girl scout, I carry my own mug in my capacious handbag. The coffee was simmering in a big tin kettle, so I figured that whatever evil might have lurked in it should have been done to death.

Half an hour later we stopped again, this time next to thick vegetation. We each selected a bush, and it was with a great sigh of relief that I climbed back on the bus – I had been beginning to regret that coffee.

Further on, rice paddies appeared. They were mostly ploughed up and lying fallow, and in one that had filled with water, large white egrets were fishing. I watched one dive his beak into the water, lift and shake a silver fish from side to side, and then swallow it. Now and then we passed a zebu cart. These oxen cattle, which are the main Malagasy source of meat, look dangerous with their long pointy horns, but are in fact docile and tractable.

We reached the open road, still in mountainous terrain, but mostly descending. The road was not wide, but it was bitumen and apart from many bumps, was good enough. There was little traffic, just trucks or bush taxis, and the odd bicycle.

This was pretty country, with stands of pine and eucalyptus trees covering the hillsides, and now and then farmhouses of rose-coloured mud brick. Long, two-storeyed and skinny, they had wooden doors and glass-less windows with wooden shutters to keep out the elements. Bricks stacked around kilns were the same colour as the earth and the houses.

Later we traversed uncultivated areas where red earth showed between gum trees, reminding me of parts of Australia. We followed a stream until it turned into a river and my enjoyment of the lovely scenery dissipated when we encountered a bridge fallen into the river. I had been warned this was common enough.

Presently we came to tier upon tier of paddy terraces, some green with young plants and some yellow with rice ripe and ready for harvest. Now and then an ancestor's tomb stood in a field, watching over the rice crop. The only animals I saw apart from zebu were three horses in a field and a couple of dogs tending the cattle.

As we approached Antsirabe, where the other four passengers were getting off, the driver told me that I would have to wait there while he got '*le probleme technique*' fixed. As we were at that precise moment hurtling down mountain roads at breakneck speed, I hoped *le probleme* was not concerned with *le brakes*.

In Antsirabe, offloaded from the bus, I took refuge from the hawkers at a table outside a nearby cafe. It was not open, but eventually a woman emerged and gave me a cup of Madagascar's good, strong coffee. I waited until the cook arrived and ordered an omelette as women with large bales of rice straw on their heads toiled past me along the road. One tried to sell me her bale. A man with an enormous clump of garlic also thought that I looked a ready buyer.

Then I had my coffee stolen! A wild-looking woman leaned over the fence that separated my area from the one next door, grabbed my cup and scoffed it down. At least it had not been my bag she coveted. The cafe owner just laughed and got me another.

The bus driver had told me at ten o'clock that he would be back in 'one hour maximum'. I was prepared for two-hour minimum, but lo and behold, after just ninety minutes he was back with an apparently healed bus. Another two hours of jolting ensued, as the road became progressively worse. Then the assistant took over the wheel and the first driver courteously asked my permission to sleep across four of the seats.

At Ambositra a taxi waited conveniently beside the spot where the bus dumped me in the dusty main street. We tootled off to find the Prestige Hotel, the resting place I had selected from my guidebook. It wasn't far, but was built on the side of a mountain and you approached it via an incredibly sharp decline. Two rows of stones had been inserted in the dirt track to keep vehicle wheels from sliding. At the bottom we came to a flat courtyard area just big enough to turn a car around in, beside which was the hotel entrance.

'Prestige' it was not. 'Quaint' was the only word for this place. Goodness knows how it had been stuck on the side of this mountain on the edge of the town. From the upstairs rooms there were views across to hillsides dotted with red farmhouses.

The woman in charge of the Prestige was verbally challenged due to a severe shortage in the teeth department – just one great yellow fang hung from the centre of her mouth – but she did her best to be friendly. Neither the taxidriver nor she could change my 10,000 ariary note, so I dumped my bag and, with the driver, set off in search of something smaller. The bank was shut so the driver went to hunt for someone rich enough to have seven dollars. It took him a long time.

I surveyed my huge new room with delight. There were two wide, many-paned windows, and double-entrance doors inset with opaque glass panels. With all its light and air, this room had a very good feel about it. There was a fireplace big enough to roast an ox in and a fine wooden bar in one corner. But I was not in the mood for a drinks party and the roasting of an ox could wait till later, so I had a nap instead.

When I crawled out of bed at six o'clock it was already dark and the hotel was deserted. The two women staff members were presumably in their living quarters, a hovel on one side of the gravel courtyard, and there seemed to be no other guests. I wandered through all the upstairs rooms, the sound of my feet on the floorboards echoing eerily through the empty building. My room had an internal door that led down into the rest of the house. Downstairs was the same. Was this the *Marie Celeste* of hotels?

Someone here had a thing for mirrors, not framed or ornate ones, but sheets of thin mirror. They had been stuck everywhere possible, on all four sides of columns and on two complete walls in what had once been the dining room, but now appeared defunct.

My room had mirrors galore too; in the main room – I won't call it the bedroom what with its bar, writing desk and sitting room furniture – as well as in the bathroom. The mirrors helped little there. The bathroom was grotty with age and disrepair and the light stayed on continuously. A patch of sticking plaster covered the switch, I presume to prevent electrocution of the unwary. The toilet trickled constantly and the water from the hand basin pipe swamped the floor. But I didn't have to worry about bathroom ventilation – a big window high on the wall had four panes for glass, three of which were innocent of that commodity. A lace curtain dragging on the floor like a slatternly negligee covered the door space.

Locking my door, which was a feat that required much fiddling and a degree in engineering, I took my torch and went looking for dinner. Forget about the American Express card, a torch is what you should not leave home without. The street was pitch black and shadowy figures brushed past me as I floundered uphill along the broken and cracked pavement.

Not far away I found a hotel that was Grand only in its name. This hostelry, according to the guidebook, was supposed to be not only quaint but replete with elderly staff. They must have all been pensioned off or gone to the Big Hotel In The Sky, because now the staff were young in the extreme. Training up the next generation, I guess.

A tiny waitress laughingly brushed the crumbs from my tablecloth with her little hand, not noticing that most of them ended up in my lap. I told her that her electric-blue nail polish was '*tres chic*'. Me and my big mouth. She reappeared with the bottle and insisted on painting my nails bright blue while I waited for my not-so-great dinner of chicken and vegetables.

Back in my room I rattled around, alone in the establishment, until bedtime when I retired to read Frank McCourt's *'Tis*, a copy of which I had chanced upon at a second-hand street stall in Naples.

The bed was comfortable, and the quiet sublime. The morning was bright and somewhere nearby a rooster was crowing. I tried to creep about when I got up at six but, worried that my feet on the bare floorboards must sound thunderous downstairs, settled on the wide balcony outside my room. Furnished with tables and chairs, it had a stone balustrade, the top of which was a planter box filled with red geraniums.

This was an exceedingly peaceful place. Above the patchwork green of the paddy fields the mist hung low over the mountains opposite. Along the mountainside to my right was a wooden, brown-painted building with a row of windows fringed by gay yellow shutters. I could tell it was a school by the chanting of little voices that came from it already by seven o'clock. In the garden below grew paw paw trees, wonderfully shaped traveller's palms and many different flowers – red and white roses, crimson azaleas, and white flowering May bushes. The garden was bordered by a type of hedge that I saw often in Madagascar – high, neat and well trimmed, a kind of conifer. The beautiful perfume of a flower floated up to me. I had noticed this scented flower in Tana. It had abundant blooms – both periwinkle blue and white growing on the same bush – that looked like small gardenia, and smelled divine, like an expensive French perfume.

I braved the bathroom and to my joy found that there was hot water in abundance, but by the time I finished I needed a boat to get out the door. There were no drains and the water from the shower simply ran onto the floor. My lairy blue nails were already chipped and I didn't have any polish remover. Then I remembered the tea tree oil in my first aid box. Marvellous stuff that fixes cuts and mozzie bites and doubles as nail polish remover – it does the lot.

At last I heard voices below. Looking over the balcony, I saw the two ladies of the house cooking breakfast on a coal-filled brazier in an alcove outside the back door.

I made a beeline for the tucker. A tiny black, white and ginger kitten played with my shoelaces while I wolfed down an omelette. Fortified by great coffee I sashayed out to see the town, and was immediately adopted by George, a young Malagasy who said he wanted to practise his English. George stuck to me like a limpet until after ten o'clock. He told me that his parents had divorced and taken off in separate directions, leaving him to care for his little sister and brother. He said that schooling was free but there was still the cost of books and uniforms. George was fortunate to have a job at a repair shop, as there is little government assistance for the poor or destitute.

We went to the post office together. I was the only customer. Shocked to discover it cost five dollars to send two post cards, I decided my friends and relatives would have to wait in vain for more after receiving this lot. Then it was on to the market, a place of low, thatch-covered stalls with food and all kinds of goods laid out on wooden benches. Off to one side, women sat on the ground with rice and grains heaped in flat baskets. They used an old food tin to measure out quantities.

George and I walked from south to north, traversing the entire town. Ambositra, although not by any means a metropolis, is a pretty town, bedecked with plants and flowers. The Malagasy grow them wherever possible – even road edges had been bordered with dark purple flowers similar to petunias. The main street straggles along for a distance, lined with a few basic shops and businesses and a couple of simple *hotelys* and hotels, one of which was uninvitingly named the Titty.

In the main street a mongrel dog sat to attention, ears pricked, beside the piece of tree trunk on the roadside that served as a chopping block for the butcher. The meat for sale lay on the open wooden counter of the shanty behind, strings of sausages looped in garlands across its front serving as decoration. I was pleased to see big meaty bones on the ground at the butcher's feet, hopefully for the dogs. The meat was zebu. The chicken I'd had last night had been a mistake. It had been as tough as old boots. I decided that from then on I would give chicken a miss and try zebu.

On the topmost hill of the town George and I came to the substantial stone church, from which I had heard the angelus ring as I got up at six that morning and, at the far end of the town, the *taxi brousse* station. I had tried in vain to locate someone who knew Madabus's whereabouts. Now I had no option for onward travel except to brave a bush taxi. It was possible to buy a ticket in advance, so I did this, arranging to leave for Fianarantsoa (Fiana), further south, tomorrow afternoon. The fare was seven dollars to reserve the entire front seat of a van for a six-hour journey. And I was not prepared to share the seat – the ride would be uncomfortable enough as it was.

The taxi station was a large open block of land – a madhouse of dilapidated vehicles parked haphazardly, with a legion of touts rushing around screaming and shouting destinations. But I was assured that all would be well with my ticket.

My shadow George proved very hard to dislodge. Later, when I emerged from the Prestige for lunch, he was waiting for me. I couldn't get rid of him without being rude, so I let him tag along. And he did prove helpful in finding the town's only phone box. Phoning was a breeze once I discovered that you have to dial '00' before the number.

I invited George to have lunch with me and we ordered what I thought was going to be a piece of fish, but we got the lot: head, tail, fins, eyes and all. It took a lot of scraping to win a little bit of flesh off the bones and I left still hungry.

Ambositra is the arts and crafts centre of Madagascar, so on my way up the street to find dinner that evening I stopped at a craft shop. There was a marvellous view over the valley from the back of the shop, so I stepped out onto the veranda. A woman asked me something and I said, '*Oui, oui*'. (Later I told myself sternly that I had to stop saying yes when I didn't have the faintest idea what I was consenting to.) Madame led me along the veranda and into a small room crammed with three long tables covered with white cloths, cutlery and glasses. Apparently I had agreed to eat there. I went with the flow and sat down. Heaven knows what I ordered, but what arrived was a very large plate with a precisely shaped mound of rice on it and another dish with some vegetables. This was the first time I had been in a Malagasy *hotely* and I had pointed to the only word I had recognised chalked on the blackboard menu: zebu. There was a suggestion of the presence of meat in the dish of vegetables; something that looked hopeful. But what lurked under the vegetables was some part of the zebu I would have preferred not to see on my plate. I think it was a foot or a knee. Whatever it was, it was inedible and only there in an ornamental capacity. The vegetables were good, however, and so was the broth that I put on my rice with lots of the chilli-garlic-ginger mixture I had become fond of.

While I was eating, five burley men indulging in a beer fest at another table did their best to get to know me. I think they were police or military. Our socialising was rather a failure due to my lack of Malagasy and their lack of sobriety, until a nice woman who spoke English appeared. She told me that the attached shop was an NGO project to help the women of the district, so I bought a wooden condiment set on the way out. Just what every traveller needs, I scolded myself as I staggered back by torchlight to my hotel, clunky pepper, salt and mustard containers on a tray.

11 Bush Bashing

After a good night's sleep, I awoke to a gorgeous morning. The kitten appeared again as I was eating breakfast, this time accompanied by its harassed-looking mother, whose tail it played with boisterously. Checking out of the hotel, I tried to pay my bill. It took the two women an exercise book and many sums, written laboriously with a pencil, to attempt the addition of two twenty-four's plus four. No agreement could be reached on the total, so I took the book and wrote the answer for them. They were amazed at my brilliance. It was sad that I'd had to live so long and travel this far for my maths to be appreciated. At school I had been as good as told not to bother any more, so I went to the beach instead of sitting the final exam. Here, there were smiles all round when my account was finally sorted out to everyone's satisfaction.

I walked downhill to the main street happily enough, but opted for a taxi to return up the sharp incline. The driver had no change. I gave him a 2000 ariary note and we agreed that he owed me a ride to the *taxi brousse* station at twelve o'clock, plus 500 change. I wondered if I would ever see him or my money again, but, true to his word, he was in the courtyard honking his horn ten minutes before the deadline and off we went.

At the station the chief passenger-procurer greeted me like a long lost friend. He escorted me, with much pomp and circumstance – all that was missing was the trumpet fanfare – to my conveyance, a battle-scarred red van of the Mazda persuasion, and seated me in style in the front seat. Expecting an imminent departure, I arranged myself as comfortably as possible. And then I waited. And waited. No one had told me that I would have to sit there until the rest of the seats were sold. Leaving at a certain time was only a hope, I soon realised, and a faint one at that.

I read my book and, between pages, watched the hectic pace of life around me. After a time, a woman and two little girls joined me in the van. Almost all the women who walked past had not only the seemingly compulsory baby attached to them, but another small child in tow. Vendors, determined to sell bananas, mandarins or small cake-like buns, pestered me. The buns were carried on a tray balanced on the vendor's shoulder where they were breathed on every time she turned her head. Wishing to give me the opportunity to share this experience, one woman shoved them in front of my nose through the window. I watched as she proffered the tray along the line of waiting vans, giving everyone a turn at sniffing and handling her offerings. Another seller of these sticky buns had a babe tied on her back who reached around every now and then, stuck his fingers in the goodies on the tray, sucked them, then put them back again. Would I like to buy one, she asked? Not right now, thank you. I've just had lunch.

Hours went by. Literally. It was half-past-two before we finally left. By this time we were fifteen adults, four children and three babies. The seat behind me accommodated all the children, one baby and four adults. Those university students who think they are so clever, squashing large numbers of bodies into Volkswagens, should see this. They might be shamed into giving up such frivolities and return to their books. Apart from a couple of wails from the wee ones, the kids never peeped. They threw up, of course, but only once copiously enough to make us stop.

We made another stop to retrieve some goods that fell off the top of the van. This did not surprise me. Tied on the van's roof was a bed, a large wooden cupboard, bags, boxes, baskets, bulky sacks, and my suitcase. Talk about a travelling circus.

Having the entire front seat to myself made me feel guilty, but I wasn't exactly throned in solitary splendour. I had the driver, his clobber, and a big container of oil under my feet. I assuaged my conscience somewhat by lifting one small child from the seat behind and putting her on the seat beside me. After a while I felt a fairy touch on my wrist and, looking down, saw a tiny finger patting my bracelet. I took it off and gave it to her. A wide-eyed little face turned to look up at me, then down to gaze, speechless, at the treasure on her wrist. Slowly a secret smile blossomed. I passed the matching one to the other little girl who was crammed between her mother's knees behind my seat. These were not exactly generous gestures. Unable to bring good jewellery with me, those bracelets were only cheap, but pretty, beads strung on elastic – a concession to the neurotic urge I have to decorate myself.

The mountainous country we travelled through after leaving Ambositra looked more fertile than around Tana, with many rice paddies blanketing the landscape. There were no towns and the villages were some way apart. Sometimes the mountainsides were clad with large stretches of pines or eucalypts, but I was dismayed to see how much clearing of the forest was happening in some places. *Tavy*, a slash and burn method of cultivation and cutting forest trees for timber, has been common practice in Madagascar for a very long time; correction of the drastic results – soil erosion, silting of rivers, and destruction of wildlife habitat – is high on the current government's agenda.

We passed small herds of zebu being escorted along the edge of the road, or pulling carts in ones and twos, as well as farmers dressed in traditional sarongs walking to and from their fields.

The road was paved and although the driver went as fast as possible, he seemed reasonably careful. As dusk fell I saw that he was getting drowsy, and kept my eye on him. Noticing this, he pulled off the road into a Shell service station, and hurried around the back. Soon he was back, looking refreshed – I didn't care to know with what.

Our van was stopped frequently at miliary or police roadblocks where we were scrutinised and our load examined, but we didn't have to get out. Usually the policemen or soldiers smiled at me and said, '*Bon jour.*'

On the outskirts of Fiana the police stopped us for the last time, and we received a thorough going over. Everyone had to stand on the road and one officer climbed on top of the van to undo, search, or prod the baggage. One of the ladies showed me in pantomime, by tipping an imaginary bottle to her mouth, that they were looking for booze. The policeman came to my bag and must have asked whose it was. A chorus of '*toureest*' answered him, at which he looked down at me. I smiled, beguilingly I hoped, up at him. Anyway, I seemed to be above suspicion, for he smiled back and moved on to the next bundle.

It was dark when we arrived in the town. A taxidriver and I stood by the side of the road with a torch and my map to decide where I should go. The first hotel I tried was full so we moved on to the next. This one, the Tsara Guesthouse, gave me a room. A fairly upmarket establishment, it came highly recommended by the guidebook. It was okay but hardly worth the thirty euros it charged. I am always suspicious of places that quote prices in a currency that is not the local one. Still, I got a great dinner there at a good price, as well as a sumptuous breakfast that, although the dreaded continental, included cheese, yoghurt, the works in fruit and buns, and even peanut butter.

Then they told me I had to leave. No, I had not managed to disgrace myself. Not this time anyway. The receptionist hadn't informed me there was only space for me for one night. So I was out on the street, homeless yet again. Muttering to myself that I didn't need their TV; that the room, although snazzy, was miniscule; and that my last hotel had given me the best room in the house with acres of space for a quarter of the price they charged for their glorified dog kennel, I used their phone to call five hostelries before I found a room. Then I got the phone bill and almost had a heart attack. No one had warned me that the guesthouse used a mobile system with exorbitant rates. Five local calls had cost twice the price of the room at the next guesthouse.

Gratefully I taxied to the Arinofy, the only place that had offered me refuge. It was suspended so high on a hill that I was sure the taxi wouldn't make the last stage of the climb up the almost perpendicular cobbled lane that led to it. Once safely there I was able to appreciate the marvellous view of the town and paddies below that its eagle eyrie position afforded. The Arinofy had bright and sunny dining and reception areas with wide-open French doors that looked out to the spectacular panorama below. But my room was a cell, basic in the extreme. And the communal loo and bathroom were primordial.

I wandered down the hill and along the main street to the post office. By the time I reached it, it was past eleven and its doors had been closed for lunch, not to reopen again until two. I had other sites in view, though. One of the reasons I had come to Fiana was that a train runs from here, in the centre of Madagascar, through the mountains, among legendarily beautiful scenery, down to the coast. Also, Ranomafana National Park is accessible from here.

Further down the main street I came to the lovely old railway station, its façade gay with boxes of red flowering geraniums lining the edge of the upstairs balcony. But the ticket office was closely shuttered, not to reopen until after lunch and siesta.

In an antique wooden railway carriage beside the station I

found a tour agent's office and enquired about a trip to the national park. The tour operator, a young woman who tried her best to help, said in the end that it was not possible. As I discovered most times in Madagascar, travel agents dealt normally with small groups, usually from France, not individuals. Later, as I was eating my lunch in a small cafe, a guide named Angelo approached me and said that word had got around that I was asking about getting to the park. I hired him, deciding he was my best option, even though he insisted we should leave at seven the next morning.

Although it is Madagascar's second biggest town and the surrounding country is fertile, producing much wine and tea, Fiana seemed a basic sort of place. Traffic was sparse and there were not many people about, especially during the two- or three-hour lunch.

Window-shopping along the street, I found the few stores a poor-looking lot, with tatty displays. Only one shop had clothing in its window, unashamedly exhibiting some horrible old stuff. Pride of place was held by a fly-blown white wedding dress that looked as though it had been cut out with a spade sometime in 1930 and stuck in this window ever since.

When the train station office reopened I found it dead easy to reserve a seat to the coastal terminus, Manakara. With a laugh, the young lady said the train left at seven o'clock in the morning on Saturday, *En'sha'allah* (God-willing). Which she was not always, I had heard.

Noticing an old hotel named Chez Papillon nearby, I went in for an inspection. Its rooms were miles better, and even cheaper, than the one I was billeted in currently, so I booked myself in for the next day. Over coffee at its street-side veranda cafe I met a Dutch couple who told me they had travelled on Madabus to Ambositra the day after I did. Their bus had broken a wheel and they'd had to wait in Antsirabe for five hours. A *problème technique*, I supposed.

Investigating the interiors of the shops when they opened, I found one that was said to be a general store. Never had a truer word been uttered. Light bulbs, canned beans, electric irons, frilly frocks, and a couple of motorbikes were on display. Another rabbit warren of a place had alcove after alcove of booty, housed in tall, narrow, glass-fronted cabinets, in front of which stood so many staff I couldn't see the contents. Their guardians wouldn't take the hint and move over.

I hiked back up the excruciatingly high hill to my guest-house and sat in a comfortable chair in the dining room where the light was good for reading. My own dungeon contained only a narrow single bed, one blanket, a cushion with a damask cover instead of a pillow, a rough table, and a shelf. But in the dining room I ate an excellent two-dollar meal of zebu steak and vegetables, then went to bed ready to do a flit in the morning.

A late arrival crashing about in the passage woke me and, much to my chagrin, I couldn't sleep again until just before I had to get up and make ready for a marathon hike around the rainforest at six!

Risen unrefreshed, I made the trek up the long passage to the loo under the gaze of two night watchmen on a couch beside my door. In my uncombed and cranky state I could not have been a pretty sight, but they remained glued in fascination as I bumbled in and out of the bathroom to complete my ablutions.

At breakfast I talked with the French girl whose late arrival had disturbed my slumbers. She had travelled all day in a *taxi brousse* that eventually had suffered a total collapse and resisted all efforts to be resuscitated until after midnight.

Angelo collected me as prearranged. I dumped my case at Chez Papillon, then he, I, and his driver departed in the usual rattletrap car. Zooming out of the town we were soon among mountains and stunning scenery on the appalling dirt track that is the only route to the east. Lurching from one almighty, tooth-loosening pothole to another, I had to hang on to the car's side strap for the next hour and a half to keep upright. Angelo told me this road was impassable in the wet season. The couple of trucks we encountered were barely moving and we travelled at a walking pace most of the time.

The scattered villages became few and far between, as did the rice paddies, until finally we were among dense forest where there was no sign of habitation. At times, except for the wild, large-bloomed pink roses that lined the roadside, the vegetation was familiar: there were gum trees and a tree with yellow blossoms, similar to Australian wattle. Angelo told me that migrating birds had brought the seeds of the trees from Australia, but I wondered whether it was because in the beginnings of time, Australia and Madagascar had both been part of Gondwanaland.

We clunked across a rickety wooden bridge high over a rushing, boulder-strewn river. Beside it, workmen were constructing a new bridge, 'because, this one is unsafe,' said Angelo. And yet, they let me be driven over it! As we reached the middle I prayed that this was not the time it chose to give up the ghost.

Further on, a boy stood by the roadside, selling live eels he had caught with a hook and line in the river. From the price – 5000 ariary – I gathered they were a luxury. He kept the eels in a cylindrical, intricately-worked rattan basket that swung from his shoulder on a string. Its shape reminded me of the knitting bags around when I was a child, in the days when every woman knitted.

At one place, sacks of charcoal for sale were lined up like soldiers beside the road. This is what people use as fuel for cooking and in braziers for warmth, creating the smoke-blackening I had seen around the doors and windows of the houses.

At last the dirt track, having climbed to a great height, changed into a new paved road and for the last fifteen minutes of the journey we went from a crawl to a flight, swerving speedily around the winding bends. If a tyre blew out, we would be sailing into eternity. Hadn't I sworn never again to travel on scary mountain roads? Funny how I only remember vows when I am doing the 'vowed not to' thing again.

At the entrance to Ranomafana National Park I took on another guide. The one who takes you there is not authorised to guide you in the park, and you can't go alone in case you get lost. My new guide, Scorpion, was an amiable young man who knew his stuff. He raced me off at a cracking pace, using thousands of toeholds worn into rocks or the earth to march me up and down the sides of slippery, moss-covered mountains and along narrow trails. The forest was dense, with giant bamboos, tree ferns and palms among the tall, thin rainforest trees. The damp foliage and bushes crowded all around, brushing me on every side. 'Watch out for leeches,' Scorpion warned. I watched!

Very soon we came upon three golden bamboo lemurs having breakfast in the trees right in front of us. I was enchanted. Lemurs were the animals I had come to Madagascar to meet. Films and photos of these gentle and attractive creatures had made me want to witness them in real life. Lemurs are found naturally nowhere else in the world except Madagascar; Ranomafana Park has twelve of the around fifty species in the country, including the golden bamboo lemur, which is found in only one other park. To come upon this trio was a bonus. These lemurs are usually hard to find. True to their name, they were gold-coloured, with thick, shiny fur like dark-yellow honey. They were about as big as a medium-sized dog with a long tail, and were feeding on bamboo shoots, their preferred diet.

Scorpion and I continued our trek through the rainforest to the sound of the bulbul and the lesser cuckoo. Now and then we came upon other tourists, including some Malagasy, who

Scorpion said were beginning to discover the attractions of their own country. For two hours we continued up and down the terrain; I saw chameleons, a rhinoceros beetle, orchids, and more lemurs – five grey bamboo lemurs, known as the gentle lemur, and two of the larger, multihued, diademed sifakas, whose exuberant colours were matched by their behaviour. They swung through the trees performing breathtaking acrobatics, as though deliberately putting on a show.

A bridge spanned a picturesque river that tumbled over large black rocks between the sides of a gorge, down which waterfalls cascaded to join it. As we crossed the bridge Scorpion told me the half dozen people working there were 'mending it'. What they were actually doing was painting the rails. I had green hands for the rest of the day.

The museum at the park gates was extremely informative; its main attraction was a live, fabulously patterned, grey, black and beige boa constrictor, curled up in a big glass case. The attendant told me it had bitten her when she took it out to clean the case. I didn't think boas bit. Although they are not poisonous – there are no poisonous snakes in Madagascar – you could still get septicaemia or tetanus from a bite.

In a nearby restaurant I decided I needed an intake of calories to recover some energy. According to a waiter, crayfish caught in the local river was the specialty. I tried some, but it was a fizzer. The crayfish were like yabbies – teeny little things, pretty to look at in their bright red suits of armour, but armour-plated was just what they were. It was almost impossible to get anything to eat out of them. I gave up and ordered a fried Camembert dish, which was great.

At the next table sat four Americans who beleaguered their guide about what the menu offered, and continued to do so in the time it took for me to order, wait for my meal, and finish eating. Stone the crows, I swore to myself, shut up, order something and eat it. These irksome people demanded to know what the fish was called, what was in the sauce, and so on. (I'm surprised they didn't ask what colour the zebu had been and what its mother's name was!)

But then I met three interesting people. From England, but now living in Cairns, they were twitchers. No, they did not have a distressing affliction; they were bird watchers, a particular breed of eccentrics that I usually get on well with. Madagascar attracts twitchers because it is home to a huge array of fascinating bird life, over 250 species, of which a great many are endemic.

By the time we returned to Fiana I was flagging, especially after another two hours on the bone-breaking roads. Thankful I hadn't attempted it in a *taxi brousse*, I fell onto the comfortable bed in my room at Chez Papillon to await resurrection.

This elderly hotel was scruffy, but had everything I needed and was superficially clean enough to be passable by my none-too-high current standards (they had dropped notches as my journey wore on). After an hour I was refreshed enough for an excursion to the town's one small supermarket. This turned out to be my sort of shop, a real Aladdin's cave. After a first-class ferret, I found a replacement coffee infuser for the one I had accidentally left plugged into the wall in Ambositra. (The staff there are probably still trying to work out what this strange bit of metal that gets hot is for. But incidentally it is a most useful thing to take travelling, for it can create coffee, tea, soup, noodles, even bath water.)

At Chez Papillon I had the usual excellent zebu steak, accompanied by a bucket of peas you could have used for artillery practice, then retired to my quarters and crashed into a sound sleep.

12 Mountain Training

The next day, boarding the train at six o'clock in the morning was a breeze. After coffee on the hotel's street-side veranda, I trundled my bag across the road, through the station building, and into the first-class carriage. The young woman who had sold me my ticket the day before was already shunting passengers into their seats. She enlisted a male bystander to lift my bag up and into the overhead rack, even ordering him to turn it around and put it the right way up.

The train was an antique piece from the 1930s. My carriage was worn and looked its venerable age, but it had been scrubbed and polished ready for the trip. I took my seat, a red leather offering that had been designed with the express purpose of keeping you uncomfortably bolt upright. My mother would have been pleased. She spent her life telling me to sit up straight.

The carriage soon filled. It had an open plan design and the seats were arranged so that four people sat facing each other. I was seated with three Malagasy and the rest of the carriage was occupied by a colourful collection of Malagasy people and nine young American students. The wide entrance doors on both sides of the carriage were left open and in the space between them, passengers who had not won a seat sat on boxes, or stood in the open doorways. This looked a perilous occupation to me. How could they fail to fly out when the train swayed violently, as it did often? There was nothing to stop them. When we reached the mountains some men even sat on the edge of the step, swinging their legs in the breeze over incredible drops to infinity.

The train set off dead on time and we clattered along, horn blaring, until we had cleared the town and outlying villages. I guessed that if folk wandered on the tracks the way they did on the roads, this was a necessity. There was only a train on alternate days and it might have come as a nasty shock to find one unexpectedly lolloping up behind you.

From then on the train stopped every half-hour or so. It was a terrific trip. I spent an entire day getting a glimpse of the life of the local people. Through the rattly old glass of the windows, most of which were permanently solidified in the half-open position, I watched freight and supplies loaded and unloaded and passengers hopping on and off.

There are no roads through the mountains. The train provides the only connection between the otherwise isolated villages and the outside world; and it must be an exciting event in some of the people's lives. Women and children stood on lonely plots of earth in front of shacks perched on mountaintops, where they waved and smiled at us. I wondered what their lives were like, and tried to put myself in their shoes for a moment.

Everyone in the carriage was friendly. As soon as we were underway, the journey became one long eating contest. Each time we stopped women and girls walked along the train windows offering food from trays they carried on their heads – bananas, loquats, pawpaw, pineapple, samosas, rice wrapped in banana leaves, and peanuts measured out with old condensed milk tins. I bought two duck eggs, hard-boiled I hoped, otherwise I was in for a fright when I peeled them. Later I added a huge hand of bananas to the cache under my seat. Be warned, you need lots of small money to travel this way. No one had change for anything larger than 500 ariary (thirty-five cents).

My Malagasy neighbour in the seat beside me was a musician. He nursed an electric guitar, which he played for me via a set of headphones. I decided that the two young Malagasy people opposite must have been on their honeymoon. They were Love's Young Dream personified. He never left her alone, leaning over to talk lovingly in her face the whole way except for when he took time off to eat. She was tiny and shy, while he was a long drink of water who needed to fold up his two-metre frame to fit onto the seat.

Our carriage collected a few extra souls along the way. Those folk stood in the aisles or door spaces, while the second-class carriages on either side of us literally overflowed. We went rollicking along, clicketty-clack, in a most satisfying real train way. Reverting to childhood, I behaved like a four-year-old. Hanging over the half open window, I put my head out in the wind, waved, shouted greetings, and generally yahooed. I did all the things railway authorities in Australia would have a fit to see you do if they didn't have the windows fixed so you couldn't. Needless to say, by the time we arrived at our destination ten hours later, I looked a right mess.

This surely must be the best rail ride in the world. The scenery was fabulous. The line ran high along the top of the mountains, sometimes going through them via tunnels. Far down below the valleys flowed away to forever, all glorious green, laced now and then by the silver thread of a river. Sometimes there were rice paddies, the water in which glittered or reflected the clear blue of the sky. There were banana plantations, and scattered here and there, tiny villages with houses that looked the size of toys, while far in the background a row of smoky-blue mountains lined the horizon. Occasionally a sparkling waterfall flashed and splashed the length of a mountainside. As I looked down on the kilometre after kilometre of country unfolding beneath me, I saw that, unlike the densely populated countries of mainland Africa and Asia, Madagascar has large, uninhabited areas where only forest covers the mountains.

Sarah, one of the American students on the train, came

to talk to me. She told me that her group had come to Madagascar for three months on a study programme organised by her school. The teenagers had been billeted in villages and the homes of Malagasy people in Tana. One girl was scratching furiously and Sarah told me that some of them had endured close encounters of the flea kind. They seemed nice kids and they did not complain, but I gathered the different life they had experienced had been a shock to them – eating nothing but rice three times a day, for example.

The train journey was exhilarating, but I was almost annihilated by a lynch mob of shoving *pousse pousse* men when I stepped onto the platform at Manakara. It was an alarming experience and if I hadn't been a seasoned lone traveller, I might have died of fright. I was grabbed, and pulled into a shouting crush of men, each determined to gain my custom. It took all my strength to struggle through them. I lunged forward, knocked off the hands that held me and, wresting my bag back from those who had seized it, turned it around and wheeled it into the mob, forcing them to make way. Other Malagasy men tried to help me but they were outnumbered and repulsed. Eventually my determined efforts got me through the worst of the scrum and outside the station to the footpath.

Slowly, still beleaguered by the pack, I continued until I found a *pousse pousse* man who sat quietly on his cart by the side of the road. Deliverance! I jumped in his conveyance and instructed him to take off fast. I was determined not to reinforce the behaviour of the others by giving them my business. I had to think of other solo travellers who might come after me.

Pousse pousse – literally 'push push' – are rickshaws pulled by a runner. I was horrified at this man-turned-to-beast-of-burden form of transport but, out of necessity and because everyone else did, I had to use it. In Asia I had always felt guilty when I made someone troll me about by the sweat of his brow, but here it was worse. At least in Asia they use bicycles.

My troubles, however, had only just begun. The driver (well, they are really runners) took me to the guesthouse that I had chosen from my guidebook. I had meant to phone ahead from Fiana to book a room, but hadn't found a phone box the previous evening and had left too early in the morning to go looking for one then. The guidebook warned there are few places to stay in Manakara and that they are often full.

I was dragged at a trot for a considerable distance, as I hadn't realised that the place I had asked for was at the beach, but found there was no room at the inn. The next place I tried was full too, so we headed back into the town. No vacancy. By now it was getting dark and I was beginning to feel like Casey Jones, destined to ride forever! Unfortunately I could blame no one but myself for the position I was now in. (To console yourself with the fact that it's not your fault always helps – but this option was not available to me.)

Pousse carts are designed for reclining in. I had my bag in front of me, my legs dangled inelegantly in the breeze each side of it, and the knobs on my bony spine were being rubbed into bedsores on the wooden rail behind me. Each time we came to a hill I called a halt and scrambled out to walk. My conscience wouldn't let this poor man drag me up a hill when I had two perfectly good legs.

Two hours later I was still homeless. It was the black of night – there were no streetlights in this town – and the prospective residences had become progressively less salubrious until finally I was in a dark street at a guesthouse so obscure it didn't even own a name. By now my driver was just taking me where he saw fit. A man loitering outside this shanty told me that I could have a room, and I decided it would have to do. A fracas with my driver ensued. He wanted half my life's blood for this ride. Even though I had walked for some of it! It didn't help that I knew the confrontation was my fault: I should not have climbed into his cart without first fixing the price. I learned this fact of life years ago when using Asian betchas and cyclos. And I found that all these men assumed the same countenance when they were overcharging you – a deeply hurt and aggrieved air that silently accuses you of being most awfully cruel to them. Now I learned that The Look was here, alive and well in Madagascar. I knew that, unless I wanted to argue all night, it was hopeless to resist once this look was levelled at me. I paid the ludicrous price, at which the villain smiled broadly and shook my hand.

Upstairs I was shown into a dingy, windowless room lit by one feeble light bulb – which immediately went out! The power was off. I groped around in my bag, located my torch and found the communal bathroom and loo. I was the only tenant in this creepy place, alone with the shifty-eyed fellow who came back with a candle and demanded money. I established that he was not the manager and the money was not for the room. He had seen me ply the *pousse* man with largesse and decided that I was a soft touch.

Suddenly I wanted out of there. I have slept in worse places, but never where I didn't feel safe with the inhabitants. My inbuilt radar tells me when the vibes are bad, and all the bells and whistles were going off here. Some people who have not travelled alone tell me that I am brave. Rubbish, I am super cautious. These same innocents trot off blithely on packaged tours that fly with local Mickey Mouse airlines I wouldn't have the nerve to board. They are the brave ones. I don't go willingly into risky situations. Anyone who demands money for nothing has suspect motives. 'No way, Jose!' I squawked, lumping my bag downstairs.

In the dark street curious men soon surrounded me, but I no longer felt threatened, just lost. I regrouped, gathered my senses and went next door where I had spotted a light. It belonged to a small *hotely* run by two women. Invoking the sisterhood, I threw myself on their charity. One woman came into the street with me, selected a *pousse* driver and spoke with him at length in Malagasy. Turning to me she explained – she spoke French but I got the gist of it – that for a reasonable sum already agreed upon, this man would take me to another, better place to sleep. Gratefully thanking her, I climbed aboard and recommenced my lost-soul wandering.

Down the street and around the corner we went and were immediately engulfed in absolute darkness on a rutted dirt track in what seemed to be the countryside. I had no idea where we were going but was not worried – if I disappeared there had been witnesses to my abduction.

We came to a hill and I climbed down to walk. Unable to find my torch, I stumbled along behind the cart. It was so dark I could see nothing, but now and then felt something move past me and discerned a vague form. Tiny, flickering pinprick lights flitted and flashed. Presumably they were fireflies, unless the mosquitoes here had taken to carrying torches. Back in the *pousse pousse*, we continued on until the next hill when I got out to walk again.

Finally, after what seemed like hours, I saw lights on one side of the track and we rolled up a long drive to a palace – or so it seemed to this homeless outcast. Many lights surrounded a white-columned patio fringed by palms and flowering bushes. An oasis couldn't have looked more appealing to a thirsting desert wanderer.

Considering the untidy arrangement of my limbs in the cart, I decided that *pousse pousse* propulsion was a most undignified manner in which to arrive at such a worthy looking place. I stopped the cart halfway up the drive and walked to the entrance, determined already that this was the end of the line. If they said they didn't have a room I would camp on the doorstep all night under the safety of their lights. I was not going back out there in the jungle.

A gorgeous, smiling young woman, who seemed not in the

least bit put off by my unsavoury appearance – I hadn't been too entrancing when I had alighted from the train and I'd deteriorated considerably since – gave me a room and told me the price was 18,000 ariary (twelve dollars). I could have fallen to my knees and kissed the hem of her garment!

Mademoiselle also told me the hotel car would have brought me from the station if they had known I was coming. *C'est la vie!*

The room was paradise after the dreadful dungeon I had been in earlier. A quick wash, dinner on the patio, and I fell into an excellent bed thanking my lucky stars and the angel who takes care of fools – there are probably a raft of them working in shifts delegated to my case – that, as Will Shakespeare said, 'All's well that ends well'.

Waking to the sound of wind soughing through pine trees and a rooster crowing, I declared the new day a holiday and decided to veg out. It was Sunday, after all.

No hot water appeared from the tap and at breakfast Mademoiselle explained that the water refused to travel upstairs. She offered me another room or, she said, she would carry hot water up for me when I wanted to wash. 'Not likely,' I replied, and decided to live with it. It was a small price to pay when everything else was so good. When the weather warmed up in the afternoon I braved the cold-water shower, but chickened out on washing my hair. That could wait until the need became desperate, which wouldn't be long. Already it was like chewing gum.

This hotel was well named the Marvela. Set in extensive grounds and gardens of green palms, pine trees, flowers and grass, the white building was old, but well cared for. Tiled patios and verandas, on which were tables for eating, drinking or whatever, surrounded its front, giving it a cool, breezy feel. I reached my room by climbing a blue-tiled staircase on the side of the building that took me onto a white-tiled balcony, which was edged with a balustrade and covered with a wooden ceiling.

My room opened off the balcony. It had a floor of polished boards and a sensational six-globe glass confection that gave a dazzling light. I had a double bed, two carved wooden armchairs covered in red velvet, and a tiny bathroom. There were embroidered doyleys and fake flowers in vases, one in the shape of a ghastly china rabbit. And I got excited when I saw two electric plugs! It took very little now to make me happy. I even had the use of a dog. A small Maltese terrier had followed me upstairs after dinner. He had stationed himself outside my door and stayed there until morning.

I was also pleased to be warm again. I had not been really cold before, but Madagascar had proved cooler than I had anticipated. Now I could wear my tropical gear and wash my one overworked jumper.

After a breakfast of eggs and coffee, I took a hike following the substantial wall that surrounded the garden, before coming to a big metal gate. Stoutly padlocked, it also had boulders piled against it to prevent it from being opened, but a little further on the wall ended in a low fence that I could climb over easily. On the other side was a dirt road that ran through scrubby bush and trees. Walking down it I saw no houses among the vegetation, only a couple of wooden huts, and I encountered no people until a couple of boys came along.

'Bon jour Madame,' they said as they passed.

The courteous Malagasy always said, 'bon jour' as they went by. And if you were eating it was always, 'bon appetite'. If I greeted them first with 'salama', I received big grins as they returned the salutation. Don't be too impressed – two weeks in the country and I had now mastered three words of the language. Only two, if you eliminate 'salama' which is from Arabic.

Mademoiselle from the Marvela and I tried to converse. She spoke French to me. I replied with English and the odd (very odd sometimes, I fear) French word and we managed. I blame the situation that no one understood much of my French on the dried-up prune of a French mistress I'd had at school. How could anyone as Teutonically-named as Fraulein Meutzenfeld bestow a decent French accent on you? Probably that's unfair. When they were giving out the gene for discerning sounds I must have been sent from the room (as I often was in French class).

The little Maltese became my constant companion. He joined me for lunch that day, and I gave him some of my chicken. He had a tough job with it, but again took up his station outside my door for the night, the little dear.

13 Beating the Bank

My room at the Marvela came equipped with mozzie-control, in the shape of a gecko. The most gorgeous shade of green, just like a tree frog, he had fire-engine red feet that looked as though he had started to paint his toenails and got carried away. Another roommate was a giant cockroach. I pulled a curtain back and there he was, level with my nose, eyeballing me. I am used to big cockroaches, but this one could have won the gold medal for body building at the Cockroach Olympics.

On this day all I managed to accomplish was to wrest some money from a bank. It would have been far easier to plan and carry out a heist. In fact, judging by the carry on I experienced at the first bank I tried, I must have looked as though I might be contemplating this deed.

Kind Mademoiselle offered to drive me to town. Off we went in a Mercedes that, from the hollow clanking under its bonnet, I didn't think would last the return journey.

Now I saw what I had travelled through in the dark on my arrival. Outside the town – that is, after you turned the first corner – there were only shacks and wooden, thatch-roofed houses scattered among the trees. Here and there people and chooks straggled over the dirt road. The roosters were a scrawny lot. A tiny bit of rooster stuck on top of ridiculously long legs, they looked like feather dusters.

Mademoiselle left me at the bank in what passed as the main street. Manakara is where the railway ends, and it looks like the end of the world: scattered houses, wide, dusty streets, no shops except a few stalls. Inside the bank I found customers sitting on a line of chairs. The Malagasy are so polite there is no need for them to stand in a queue. You put the papers for your transaction on the counter in an orderly row and you are served in due sequence. I waited half an hour for my turn to come up only to be told that I needed the numbers of all my traveller's cheques to cash one. Because the numbers are – for security – on a separate piece of paper, and you are not supposed to carry the two together, I did not have them with me. This was the first time in all my travels that I had ever been asked for this document. By now it was almost eleven, the bank's closing time, so I moved on.

I clambered into a *pousse pousse* and headed out to the beach, where the Hotel Pangales sounded a good place to have lunch. On the way I spotted the other bank the town boasted, the Bank of Africa. I had cashed a cheque at their head office in Tana, so I popped in to try my luck there. The charming cashier said that he would have to phone Tana for authorisation, took my passport, and told me to come back after lunch at two o'clock.

The Pangales is a collection of small bungalows, well-spaced between gardens and trees, in a great location right on the beach. Beside the hotel was a big swimming pool. Because of the dangerous currents and sharks, it is not recommended you swim in the sea along this coast. I wandered through the hotel's empty bar and sat in the equally vacant restaurant, looking out to a sea covered with rollers that roared in from the Indian Ocean and smashed on the sand almost at my feet. Out there, I mused, was Australia.

After an hour of this, I began to feel that I had found another *Marie Celeste* of the hotel world. At last a man appeared and told me the bar and restaurant were closed today: I would have to leave.

Ejected yet again, I wandered the street and found a *pousse*

pousse man who agreed to take me back to town to the Flamboyant, another alleged supplier of vittles. This driver, as opposed to the other one, asked me for 1000 ariary – seventy cents was apparently the going rate. And surprisingly, at the end of the ride he didn't ask for more. I was so pleased I gave him a sizeable tip.

At the Flamboyant the proprietor left her washtub to tell me cheerfully that she needed three hours notice to feed me. What were they going to do, build the ruddy kitchen? She directed me across the road. This humpy, masquerading as a restaurant, only served food after five o'clock. A girl could starve here. Next door I found an even more basic establishment, but in this one the folk were super friendly and agreed to provide me with fodder.

After due consultation with the cook/waitress/manager, I ordered fillet of fish (I hoped – the menu was a mixture of French and Malagasy) and sat at a table by the side of the road. Soon school came out and many children sauntered past. One little boy stopped to stare at me and before long there were a dozen juvenile voyeurs hanging over the low paling fence goggling at my peculiarities. Western travellers are still a novelty in Manakara.

It took an age for anything in the way of food to appear, but the fish was delicious and there was no sign of fins or tail. As I was finishing, I saw the cook's assistant strolling back from up the street swinging a plastic bag that contained the baguette that should have been the accompaniment to my fish. This was presented to me, but I had closed my stomach and no longer wanted it. The children asked me if they could have it so I shared it among them.

The railway station was supposed to reopen after its three-hour siesta at two o'clock, so I decided to go there and book on the next train back to Fiana, in two days time. A *pousse* man seemed to understand where to take me but, after travelling a long way, we landed at a riverside restaurant that he had apparently concluded would be a good place for me – although he knew I had eaten lunch. By now the whole town knew what I was up to. We were near the bank, so I stopped there. It was shut, but was due to open in ten minutes – or forty, as it turned out. However, they had gained permission to give me my cash and I clumped out with money belt stuffed full, looking as though I was expecting again.

As I was being hauled along the dusty road to the station, we passed a man strolling in the opposite direction. My driver hailed him. Changing course, he walked beside me and asked where I was going. With great difficulty we established that I wanted to buy a ticket on the train. He continued beside me until we reached the station and then disappeared – until the shutter of the ticket counter rolled up and there he was again. This gent was the officer in charge. If I hadn't met him on the road there would have been no one there to sell me a ticket.

Then I bumped back over the track to my hotel. When I had begun giving the driver instructions, he shushed me with nods and smiles. He didn't have to be told where I was staying. I estimated that the trip was about two kilometres. When we came to the hills and hard bits, I plodded along beside him in the dirt.

In my room I washed my flea-bitten legs. Would I never learn? After previous disasters of this nature, it should have been engraved on my heart that upholstered chairs were suspect when the establishment harboured cats and dogs. Mozzie and sandfly bites are nothing compared to flea bites. And these were the Real McCoy. Red, angry lumps as big as fifty-cent pieces covered the back of my thighs, and the burning irritation from them was intense. One patch where I had scored several hits on the same spot was the size of a tennis ball. All I could do was wash the bites and put tea-tree oil or tiger balm on them every few hours. During the night the itch again became intolerable and I had to get up and repeat the operation.

I was the only guest at the Marvela and it was wonderfully quiet, except in the early evening when the staff and assorted hangers-on congregated downstairs in the veranda restaurant to watch a hideous soap opera that was all shouting, screaming and violence. The beautiful cool mornings were especially peaceful. As I waited for breakfast on the patio, I watched a lad cleaning the floor tiles of the veranda, pushing half a coconut husk back and forth rhythmically under one foot, then the other. The husk is fibre and when cut in half the fibres fray and make a perfect non-abrasive scourer.

I wondered what they got up to in that kitchen. After twenty minutes or so someone would bring a tray. I would sit up eagerly, taste buds agog, teeth at the ready, but the tray brought only salt, pepper and a napkin. After half an hour or more coffee would arrive. Only much later came the food.

After my night of contending with my gigantic flea bites, I had a totally relaxed day writing, reading and resting and was up at five the next brilliant morning, ready to leave for the train at six. Mademoiselle's father, a tall, distinguished-looking Malagasy gentleman who was the local doctor, drove me to the station in the battered Merc. I shook his hand and trundled my bag onto the platform. A far more dignified exit than my arrival in the midst of that awful rugby scrum.

In front of me Two Fat Ladies of the French variety were attempting to board the train. One had a walking stick and was pretty decrepit. It took three of us to heave her onto the carriage, one pulling and two below with our shoulders to the wheel, hoisting. I didn't care to think about her attempting to use the train's loo. It was difficult enough for able-bodied souls like me in a jolting swaying train, but I gave her a gold star for travelling anyway.

There were many local people on the train and a handful

of French tourists. We shot out of the town with all possible honking and show, and barrelled through the flat land near the coast where workers were already hard at it in the paddy fields. They seemed to do most of the ploughing and other work by hand, using hoes, rakes and pitchforks. Only once did I see a zebu pulling a plough. I guessed the train was belting along in order to prepare for the time it would lose when we climbed the slopes ahead. The mountains slide down abruptly from the plateau above and there is only a narrow strip of coast on this side of the country. I was enchanted by the flowers growing beside the track, which glowed in the bright morning sunshine: red and yellow canna lilies, purple morning glory, red poinsettias, yellow and mauve lantana.

The first few stops were brief, depending on the cargo to be collected or off-loaded. At one place a pile of chattering, laughing schoolchildren climbed aboard to ride to the next station.

Soon we started to climb. In this steeper terrain, the paddy fields had to find space in narrow clefts and valleys between the sides of enfolding mountains. My second train ride, instead of being more of the same, was a new delight. Whole communities rushed out to greet us, children of the small villages all barefoot. In bigger places, a few wore rubber thongs, but none were well dressed, some boys wore nothing but tattered shorts. Many villages looked mean and poverty-stricken, made up of hovels inhabited by thin, poorly-clad people.

Once we stopped on the top of a mountain and were met by a line of the most ragged-looking people I had seen on this journey. They stood by the side of the track on the edge of a precipitous drop. I wondered why the train had come to a halt here until I saw the engine driver collect a couple of live chooks and some sacks of cassava from these folk and load them into his engine compartment. Some passengers also bought fowls along the way from women who held them up under our eyes for inspection as we hung out of the windows. I decided I didn't fancy a live hen right then.

The cuttings between mountainsides were so narrow that sometimes there were only centimetres to spare on each side of the train, and now and then they were so deep I could not see to the top of the mountains. The train thundered into the many tunnels through mountains and roared out the other side with a tremendous noise.

I bought eggs from villagers again, so freshly boiled they were still warm. I wasn't game to try the sausages, meatballs and vivid pink shrimps that progressed along the line of carriages. I would have loved to, though, but didn't fancy getting sick.

One young French traveller in my carriage amused the village children with paper aeroplanes, which were obviously new to them. They chased after them, squealing and laughing. No wonder all the kids from each place waited eagerly for the train.

A very shy Malagasy boy of about ten sat across the way from me with his parents. When a village woman came aboard and there was no seat for her, the boy gave her his seat and later, when the one beside me was vacated, he sat there. He carried a tin pannikin and one of the large French ladies put some Coca-Cola in it. For a long while he sat staring intently at the bubbles in the mug. Eventually, greatly daring, he put the mug to his lips, but still he didn't drink. Finally he took a sip. It didn't bite or burn as he had expected, so he took another. Then he swigged the lot. Another new addict!

Occasionally the train track became a double line. One train came every other day from each end. About halfway into our journey we met the train that had left Fiana that morning, producing much shouting and hilarity as we passed. It was great fun.

A young man joined the carriage with his fighting cock – a fine, well-fed, autumn-toned bird. He treated it like a baby, holding it, stroking its glossy plumage and taking it on the platform for a walk when we stopped at stations. It behaved admirably, never attempting to run off, remaining by his side like a faithful dog. Now and then the man took corn from his pocket and the bird ate from his hand. But from the moment it was put on the floor under his owner's seat at midday, it commenced crowing every few minutes of the journey. Spoiled brat or punch drunk? Once, when the fighting cock was on a station platform for R & R, a rooster took him on. This local boy, a bedraggled white bird, was scrawny but as game as Ned Kelly. I think he would have had the best of the contest if the pampered one's owner had not picked up his pet and retreated from the fray. Fortunately neither got hurt, as they had no murderous blades attached to their spurs. I was pleased to see the local rooster got the corn that was left behind.

Finally the long pull up the mountains was over, and we came down the other side, an iron horse at full gallop, in a motion of two very fast heaves followed by a forward lurch. Now and then we stopped to cool the brakes, or so I thought. Hoped, in fact.

The train arrived at Fiana on time. It doesn't often I believe. The one the next day was more than two hours late. So I do win sometimes. The arrival melee wasn't too bad and I clattered my bag across the road to the Papillon, where I was told that, no, they didn't need to go through the business of registering my passport again as now they knew me. How comforting.

14 The Meaning of Life

Back at the Papillon, there was time for a rest before evening. I had to resort to the bedside Bible for reading material. It was the only book I found in Madagascar that was written in English. It was in French and German as well – thank heaven the Gideon cover all contingencies. I had finished my last book, 'Tis, and was desperate for something to read. But I was also eager to read the Bible. Frank McCourt had aroused my curiosity by saying in 'Tis that he had a friend who swore that the explanation of the meaning of life was to be found in the Gospel of St John. Now that was a claim that simply had to be investigated. It's not everyday you get the chance to find the meaning of life.

When sufficiently renewed, I walked to the town's supermarket to stock up on emergency rations for my onward travel – and found myself in the Demon Drink aisle. I hadn't touched a drop since Italy, except for a small sample of the local red wine at the Marvela. It had been drinkable, but weak. Here I found that rum is the liquor produced and, obviously preferred, in Madagascar. There were three shelves of it – a fascinating array of brands and bottles, all of them preposterously cheap. Deciding it was obligatory to try the local creation, I read my way along and finally selected a white rum called Casanove. This paragon claimed to be not only superior, but also exclusive and definitely the best. It was the most expensive too, at one dollar sixty for 750 millilitres.

Back in my room I tried the Casanove with some Coke,

one can of which had cost as much as the entire big bottle of the hard stuff. Wow! That jungle juice was white lightening! I hardly made a dent in the bottle, but there was no way I could have drunk more. I felt terrific though. I waltzed gaily down the stairs to the dining room. The waiter caught me at the bottom, set me right-side-up again and steered me into a chair. I had a bit of trouble with the menu; I couldn't understand why they had printed it all wavy like that. An excellent two-dollar zebu fillet mignon later I fell into bed with St John, but he was wavy too so I gave up. The meaning of life would have to wait. Watch this space!

In the morning I read more of the rum label. It said, in red letters (for danger?), that it was forty per cent proof. Casanove also bragged that it had won a gold medal in 1882 at Bordeaux, but that was a very long time ago and I imagine there has been a lot of water through the factory since then.

Across the road in the old railway carriage that served as the tour operator's office, I learned that Madabus called in there at six that night on its way back to Tana. It was that or a bush taxi, so I bought a ticket to Antsirabe, a town en route said to be attractive and have interesting colonial buildings. From a phone box at the post office I tried to make a room reservation in that town, but the operation proved a dead loss. The numbers were wrong, changed, or gave me recorded messages. I left a communication on one of these, booking a room (I hoped). While at the post office I bought a postcard, then discovered that the box to post it in was located two buildings down the street and up a flight of stairs. I had to ask directions twice to find it.

After checking out of the Papillon at noon I had six hours to wait until the bus left. I sat at the bar of the Papillon for a while, stretching the limits of my French with the barman, then moved to the veranda cafe where a small boy tried to sell me some vanilla pods. He had bundles of about ten, costing three Australian dollars each. I knew that, as the government tightly controls the sale of vanilla in order to obtain all the revenue, this would have to be black market produce. Even if I had wanted to buy it, I wouldn't have been able to get it past our beagle Customs' doggy in Adelaide. But it did smell heavenly.

Vanilla found its way from Mexico to Madagascar, via Europe, in 1873. A genus of orchid well suited to the climate of the country's tropical north-east, it flourished and for a while Madagascar was the world's leading producer of vanilla. Now, Madagascar shares the title with Indonesia. Vanilla is vital to the country's economy; Coca-Cola, the world's biggest buyer of vanilla, switched to synthetic vanilla for a period in the 1980s, causing a downturn in the country's finances.

Slow-growing and one of the earth's most labour-intensive crops, vanilla is expensive and the price is now high enough to make it desirable to smugglers. The trail that leads from the north-eastern part of the country, known as the Vanilla Coast, is dubbed Smuggler's Way, and murders and robberies frequently occur along it.

I had become firm friends with the lovely girl who worked in the travel agent's office in the old railway carriage. As I waited there for the bus I showed her my photos of Manakara which were stored in my notebook computer. Oh, the wonders of the twenty-first century! The ability of this little machine impressed even me, devout Luddite though I am. We exchanged email addresses and I discovered her name was Jamila. When I said, 'That's Arabic for beautiful,' she told me that she was Muslim, but didn't wear the *hijab* to work.

'My father is not so strict about such things,' she added. 'But I do observe the prayers and fasting.'

When the bus arrived, only three quarters of an hour late, Jamila said, 'Now I will kiss you.'

'Okey dokey,' I agreed.

I wasn't one to complain about a bit of kissing. The Malagasy acquired this habit from the French and like the French they go overboard and it's a kissy kind of place.

Although the bus was full, I found a seat at the back next to a pair of Polish brothers who had been riding bicycles around the countryside for three weeks. They said they had felt threatened in the sapphire mining towns of the south, but otherwise it had been a good experience. Madagascar has a great wealth of precious sapphires, another commodity supposedly controlled by the government, that is also smuggled and sold illegally. The south-west apparently is another Wild West kind of place like the Vanilla Coast. A Malagasy official is said to have claimed the country could write off its national debt with the money raised from selling just twenty kilograms of sapphires, but that most of the gems are pirated out of the country. They certainly are not for sale to tourists. I hunted the shops for sapphires, but saw only a few small, inferior stones.

The bus set off, performing the usual number of stops every five minutes before finally getting underway. Ours was a careful driver, but still I was relieved that in the darkness I couldn't see the frightening drops down mountainsides. At half-past-nine we stopped for food in a village *hotely*. I ordered chicken soup, which turned out to have had only a brief acquaintance with any form of poultry. But there was a bone of some unidentifiable animal's leg in the bottom of the bowl.

The toilet was a great distance away. I felt my way in pitch dark along a cobbled lane, then down some steps and along even more paths. The only good thing about this toilet was that it was a very long way from the kitchen. As on previous travels, I suffered penis envy as I saw the male passengers shun the dunny's pungent aroma and head for the bushes.

At two in the morning, several hours late, we arrived in Antsirabe. I was the only passenger to get off here. Dumped by the side of a dark road, I descended from the bus into a howling gale of *pousse pousse* men. I chose one and this worked wonders. The others immediately fell back. But when he and I agreed to a fare of 5000 the rest of the crowd all collapsed with laughter.

It was a long way to the guesthouse where I had made a supposed reservation via the recorded message. It was locked up tight as a drum and appeared deserted. Defeated, I let the *pousse* man take me where he wanted, the Hotel La Casa. It looked okay. A bell on the gate summoned the watchman and accomplice and we all stood about while I argued with the *pousse* man, who now wanted much more than 5000 ariary. I noticed that the other men didn't take sides, but one gave me a surreptitious nod when I said that this was enough. At last I paid three times the price and we shook hands all round.

I was ushered into an upstairs room, which was clean with a decent bed and an enormous bathroom. It seemed to be one or the other when travelling: bathrooms either fitted like a glove or were the size of a ballroom. But there was evidence of warm water in this one; in the bedroom a monstrous hot water system stood guard over the bed like a menacing metal angel.

That night I had difficulty falling asleep straight away. The occupants in the room above were working their way through the Kama Sutra. I slept for only three hours and then was woken by two raucous roosters having a crowing competition under my window. Soon, however, the shouting and shrieking of what sounded like several thousand children obliterated the roosters' racket. This excited a couple of dogs into joining in the bedlam. The noise stopped as the school next door assembled and then I heard the children singing, which was a whole heap better.

But now I had no hope of returning to sleep. I prised open my eyes and test-drove them around the room. They seemed to be still working, so I got up. The shower was great and through the gaps between the louvres I could see the pretty garden below. Also people. I was dreamily contemplating the scene when I suddenly realised that if I could see the passers-by, they could see me! (Albeit only in slices between the louvres and hopefully not the interesting bits.)

Coffee, and lots of it, and I was off to do the town. At the gate another gang of *pousse* blokes compressed me. I chose one and enlisted the hotel gateman as a witness that he had agreed to take me to the town centre for the going rate. Pointless exercise! When we arrived he demanded five times as much. I was fed up with this constant hassling. I like a quiet life. I decided to do away with the need for rickshaws by moving uptown.

I checked out the very central Green Park Guesthouse, found it fabulous and available and returned to pack my bag and leave. The management of the Hotel La Casa was not amused at my flight and even though I had not overstayed checkout time, they charged me for the room for that day. Still the move was worth it. I was thrilled with the refuge I had found.

The Green Park had been recommended by the writers of the guidebook, whose judgement, in my opinion, had not always proved to be infallible. They had raved about the Tsara Guesthouse in Fiana, which I hadn't been mad about, but this time they were right. In fact, Green Park was much better than they gave it credit for. It was a little gem.

Waiting for my room to be ready, I sat on the balcony of the attached restaurant, half asleep. After a while unease entered my daydream and I realised that somewhere in the distance a cat was meowing. Now why should that cause me disturbance? I mused. Suddenly I shot up like a skyrocket. I was sitting on a cushion that a cat may have been near – a potential for flea bites! It had taken me a while, but even I eventually learn from my mistakes.

Green Park's remarkable feature is that its rose-red brick bungalows are completely round. Crowned with circular tiled roofs rising to a pointy peak, they are set apart and private, screened by hedges and curved garden walls. Surrounded by flowering bushes, they nestle among delightful grounds dotted with ponds and pools. These produced masses of mosquitoes, but I was enchanted with my bungalow. I had never slept in a circular room before. At last I had made it into an ivory tower. The windows and doors also reminded me of a fairytale castle. Rustic to the last degree, they were arch-shaped, had frames of rough wood and were closed by pulling their outside shutters. There were two doors, one to enter and one that opened onto a tiny balcony.

The brickwork inside my bungalow was painted flamingo pink, the floor was tiled and the ceiling was wooden. It was frugally furnished – you can't stand much furniture against a round wall – but ledges at various places substituted admirably. A curtain across one section of the wall partitioned off a minute bathroom where, for an obscure reason, the shower and loo were elevated on a tiled platform half a metre off the ground, necessitating an athletic leap to reach them.

I pulled open my balcony door and stepped out. Down below, a mass of pink and mauve waterlilies floated on ponds, which lay peacefully under a curved bridge. The ponds were surrounded by green lawns dotted with blue, white, mauve and crimson flowers and small, thatched gazebos. All this cost twelve dollars per bungalow regardless of the number of occupants.

15 Blowout in a Brousse

The next day, out walking to discover Antsirabe, I decided this town looked more like a capital city than Tana did. With its grand nineteenth-century French colonial buildings, wide, palm-lined boulevards and shady arcades, it appeared to me much more important. Originally founded by Norwegian missionaries, who liked its cool, healthy mountain climate, Antsirabe was chosen later as a hill station by the French, who established a spa at the nearby therapeutic springs. The missionaries are still there – not the originals, of course – and their organisation still run the local hospital.

I thought the post office and railway station buildings lovely, even though the latter is only for show, for trains no longer operate here. Many of the once fine houses were empty and decaying, however, or in use but not cared for. The Antsirabe Bureau d'higeine, located in one of these houses, was not a good advertisement for its professed services. Looking far from hygienic, it had broken shutters falling askew on their hinges, walls stained with mildew, and grounds that were a mess of weeds and rubbish. I decided that if this lot were overseeing the sanitation, it did not bode well for the town's health.

That night I ate in the Green Park's restaurant. The food, when it finally appeared, was excellent, and the bill was presented to me in a pretty, locally made wooden box.

The sun woke me in the morning, flowing in through the

glass of the balcony door. From my bed I could see the garden, the glittering water in the ponds, the rustic bridge and the bright flowers. It was a lovely way to wake up.

After breakfast I went to explore the town further. I followed the main street, which was lined with many small shops and leads to the bustling market crammed with food stalls. I came upon the pharmacy and, approaching its worn wooden counter, I asked for some aspirin and was given a sheet of ten tablets in an unwrapped foil pack. The cashier, marooned in his glass cage at the other end of the counter, used an adding machine to deduct 1000 from the 2000 ariary note I handed him and seemed amazed to find the answer was 1000.

Back at the Green Park I met Michel, a tour guide, and with him arranged the hire of a car and driver to visit two local attractions, both lakes in old volcano craters. The car turned out to be a bucket of bolts, a decrepit Renault in the last stage of exhaustion, that needed to stop several times during the day for loving ministrations from its owner.

After leaving the town we stopped for petrol and took onboard spare fuel, in two plastic lemonade bottles that nestled alongside me between the front seats. On the outskirts of Antsirabe we passed the Three Horse Beer factory, the local beer I had seen advertised everywhere simply as THB. The other sign that dominated advertising was Tiko, the yoghurt company owned by the president of Madagascar, Marc Ravalomanana, a handsome gent whose portrait graced every bank and post office.

The road was an awful wreck. As we crawled along in a cloud of dust, the only other vehicles I saw were bicycles and zebu carts. We overtook and passed one cart, but only just. We weren't going much faster than it was. No speed records were broken this day – it took five hours to cover seventy kilometres. We bumped and rattled through villages containing the usual surfeit of children. It was Saturday and they were out of school and playing, some with wooden bocce balls, in the dust of the streets.

The first of the volcanic lakes, Lac Andraikiba, is vast and is said to be haunted by the ghost of a girl who drowned there. Half its banks had been denuded of trees to accommodate fields, and this detracted in a depressing way from its appeal. On one side of the lake a row of stalls offered jewellery alleged to be gemstones, along with items carved from natural stone which were undoubtedly real. I couldn't resist a bunch of amethyst grapes.

The second lake, Lac Tritiva, is also thought to be haunted, this time by two lovers who, thwarted in their marriage plans, leapt into its waters from the cliffs high above. It is *fady*, taboo, to swim in this lake, a deeply hidden and rather eerie place that I had to descend on foot down a long path to reach.

I cannot say truthfully that I enjoyed the ride to the lakes, but in places the scenery was stunning. From great heights I looked down, as if through a kaleidoscope, on valleys of rice and vegetable plots.

I ate in the Green Park restaurant again that night and ordered 'Fish Surprise'. The surprise turned out to be that there wasn't any fish. It took the waiter thirty minutes to establish this fact. I ordered pizza instead. The big brick pizza oven was right there in the room with me so I could watch as three boys spent over an hour fiddling with my meal.

The pizza was scrumptious, although I was expected to eat it with a knife and fork. I believe pizza needs to be eaten with your hands. It just doesn't taste the same using cutlery. I guess this refinement is another French legacy. The French are far too cultured to eat like we do, shovelling food barbarously in our faces with our grubby paws. They use eating irons for everything. On the ship I had watched, fascinated, as a young officer peeled his prawns with a knife and fork. No mean feat that. A surgeon at work with a scalpel could not have been more precise.

After a good night's rest, the next day I breakfasted at a cafe in the main street where I was served an *'Omeleete Surprize'*, but it was perhaps no surprise that the contents looked like last night's leftovers. This suited me just fine. It was a good meal of onions, cheese, fish, and ham – whatever had come to hand in the kitchen.

But going to this part of the town was a pain. Each time I did so, *pousse pousse* men and beggars assailed me on all sides. I had to give the beggars all my small money in exchange for them leaving me alone, which I suppose was their aim. One woman asked me for a T-shirt and followed me back to the guesthouse when I said I'd see what I could find for her. When I came back out I gave her a pair of my slacks that had fallen on hard times. Later I found it rather strange to see something that had been a part of my life begging on the street.

The next day, Sunday, was again a day of rest for me. There wasn't much else to do. The morning dawned balmy and beautiful and I took a delightful walk in the mild sunshine through the quiet streets of the almost empty town. Near the post office a stall had been set up for roadside breakfasting under the leafy canopy of a spreading tree. A wooden table held bowls containing noodles and another line of bowls had an array of items to add to them. The use of the peanut was big here and several women sat on the ground with mounds of them in rattan baskets ready to sell. I watched one woman's two tiny and extraordinarily soiled children doing this job with filthy hands and accompanying dribbles.

As I walked back to the hotel, a beggar woman who regularly accosted me approached. For the first time I looked closely at the child she always carried on her back. It was about twelve months old and laughed and waved its little hands joyfully, unaware of what life had in store for it. I was overwhelmed with pity for the wee innocent thing. In the busiest part of the town every day I saw a young child, probably about three years old, who was left alone to beg, sitting on a piece of rag in the middle of the footpath among the feet of passers-by. Unspeakably dirty, but with an angelic face and a mop of curls that made Shirley Temple look like an old boot, this child sat there all day, every day, from early morning until late. She never complained. Sometimes she was curled up on her rag, sound asleep. I decided that a woman who sat with another child far away on the opposite side of the broad street must have been her mother. The cathedral was nearby. I popped in for a quick request. Help! Send someone to rescue these children!

The cathedral's interior was fantastic. Many wonderful blue and white vaulted ceiling arches crossed the wide main body of the church and down both sidewalls a row of magnificent stained glass windows marched in a line to the altar. From my room at the Green Park I had heard the cathedral's bells ringing the angelus – a familiar and comforting sound. Whenever I hear the angelus I am reassured that nuns are still being called to chapel, and the faithful to prayer, at six in the morning and evening. The angelus can still be heard in countries not controlled as yet by the noise police and it is good to know that some things continue despite progress.

The next morning I was up and ready early for the trip back to Tana. I'd had the option of Madabus in the middle of the night or a *taxi brousse* and chose the latter. At the bank where I went to try to cash a traveller's cheque, Madame, the cashier, was enthroned behind a half-moon shaped desk and we, the hopeful petitioners, arranged ourselves around it on a semi circle of chairs. The man next to me soon got up and moved, due no doubt to the embarrassing odour of old wet socks that emanated from my bag. It contained a baguette I had prepared for my journey, filled with cheese made by the monks and nuns of the local monastery, delicious but very pungent. I had come prepared for this bush taxi journey, alleged to be a four-hour job, that could take all day. I had seen *taxi brousse* broken down by the side of the road and their passengers standing around forlornly. I might end up forlorn, but I was not going to be hungry.

At the *taxi brousse* station I was immediately seized by a man who sold me the front seat of a van. The rest of the seats filled up quickly and we left at half-past-nine, trundling away from the hawkers selling loquats.

The passengers behind me weren't so crushed this time, so I did not feel as guilty about my sole occupancy of the front seat. Soon we were speeding down sweeping curves and sharp corners, our tyres shrieking in protest. Wishing I hadn't jettisoned that rum at the last hotel, I consoled myself that there was one good thing about this trip. The stereo was broken. It failed to cooperate no matter how much the driver bashed it.

I will not go into tedious detail about my terror during the journey, but it peaked with a huge explosion, a wild skid, and a screeching stop on the verge of the road. Fortunately we had not been on a mountain edge.

We passengers milled about in the road while the driver's assistant speedily changed a shredded tyre. His expertise must have come from much practice. My precautions against roadside starvation proved unnecessary. In a few minutes a stream of vendors materialised to offer us bananas, loquats and skinny barbecued chickens in open rattan baskets (I chose bananas). We were not far from a village where *taxi brousse* usually stopped.

We continued on, this time not as fast on corners. I think we were on our last spare tyre. The window on my side of the van was missing and, although it was a lovely day, clouds of dust blew in on me. Later when I washed my shirt the water turned dark brown. I always started out looking squeaky clean, and ended up a mess no matter how hard I tried to stay presentable.

We must have been stopped more than a dozen times at military, police or gendarme checkpoints. We were inspected by soldiers with rifles, police wearing side-arms and waving guns, and by gendarmes, also well-armed and wearing those hats affected by the French police that have tops the shape of a camembert cheese. They were checking for smuggled goods, drivers without permits – and collecting bribes to augment their salaries.

The road passed through valleys covered with vegetable plots, some of them under harvest. Long rows of bright, shiny, newly dug carrots were heaped for sale in large orange mounds by the roadside. Another spot had pineapples and papaws.

The ride – all 170 kilometres of it – only took the four hours promised. It is a wonder that *taxi brousse* can make these times given how much they have been thrashed.

Coming into Tana took a while. It is spread out, with extensive scruffy outskirts. On arrival I had several offers of a taxi even before I climbed out of the van. Battered and tired, I had lost all resistance and allowed a tout to kidnap me. His friend gave him 200 ariary for winning me from the scrum, I was then ripped off for twice the price agreed upon at the other end. In Indonesia or Vietnam for example, once the bargain is made, it's adhered to. But here, no deal. This was Madagascar's only failing.

Heading for the Shanghai Hotel again, the taxi entered the street from the other end – the one that was nearer the US embassy – and the inspection took six soldiers with guns and metal detectors to clear me for entry.

It was great to receive a warm welcome at the hotel. Suddenly remembering that I wouldn't be able to cash money where I planned to go next, I rushed to the bank. Here I received an unpleasant revelation. They had another new rule. They wouldn't cash American Express traveller's cheques without, not only the piece of paper with all the numbers, but also the original receipt from the issuing bank. Mine was safe – in my desk in Adelaide. I dashed back to my suitcase to see if there was something in there that would help. It was now half-past-two and the bank closed again at half-past-three. I could find nothing except a receipt from this particular bank for the cashing of a previous cheque. I offered it. With no result! This was getting serious. Traveller's cheques were my only means of acquiring money here. There are no ATMs or credit card facilities. I asked to see the manager.

In due process I convinced the manager and his assistant, who both interrogated me for an hour, that I was not about to defraud them. Why didn't American Express tell you that the receipt was what you don't leave home without? The manager told me that the bank had recently been robbed of several thousand dollars. They had cashed fake Amex cheques and this was why they had instituted the new policy.

Flush with ariary and refusing to think about how any future attempts to liberate my money from banks might fare, I jumped into a taxi and went to Madabus, where I bought a ticket to Andasibe for the day after next. East of Tana on the road to the coast, Andasibe is near the Parc National de Mantadia where I hoped to see more lemurs.

The following morning I had breakfast under the bougainvillea vine in the Shanghai's garden. It was now perfect spring weather. Occasionally a papery purple flower drifted from the vine to land with a gentle rustle on the piece of paper I was writing my to-do list on.

By four o'clock that afternoon I had done only one of the three simple things I had written on the list. I had tried unsuccessfully to phone ahead to Andasibe to book a room. I had tried to ring home – also a fizzer. But I did triumph over the internet. This was enough. I gave up on the others.

I had only one slight hiccup getting to Madabus early in the morning. The taxidriver vowed he knew where to take me after the hotel night watchman had given him instructions, but he was halfway to the *taxi brousse* station in the opposite direction before I stopped him. We turned around, found the right place and I climbed gratefully into the bus.

16 Lemurs at Last

The bus took an hour to clear the town and its outskirts. At first sight I had thought Tana wasn't much chop but it grew on me, especially the pleasing buildings, parks and churches in the areas away from the Basse Ville. As we headed due east beyond the town I spotted one lone hawk, hovering over a rice paddy, in search of his breakfast.

The road wound up into the mountains and we zigzagged swiftly along the escarpment at the end of the plateau and entered thickly forested hills, sprinkled with stands of eucalypts and pines, and only an occasional village. We crossed countless streams and a couple of big rivers, in some of which women were washing clothes. Then the villages ceased and the forest became even thicker.

The bus ride was a breeze compared with the scary bush taxis. Onboard with me were five young travellers, two French and three German, the latter students in Madagascar to study the carnivorous pitcher plants. After a long drive we passed through Moramanga, a good-sized town serviced with hotels and restaurants.

Thirty kilometres later and three hours after we'd left Tana, we stopped. This bus trip terminated at Toamasina on the coast and that's where I would have been carried if, when the bus made its first stop, I hadn't asked where we were. It didn't look like the Hotel Feon'ny Ala, the place Madabus's agent in Tana had told me was the drop-off spot for bus passengers for Andasibe. The driver assured me I was going to Toamasina.

I managed to convince him otherwise, but we had passed the Hotel Feon'ny Ala's entrance a kilometre or so back. We were now at the information office at the entrance of the Parc National de Mantadia, so the driver took me to the only other accommodation alternative on the road, the Hotel Buffet de la Gare, two kilometres further on.

This, the railway refreshment room and hotel, had been built right on the station platform. A huge 1930s relic from the glory days of train travel, it reminded me of a grand European country house. Here I was granted sanctuary, but only for one night. They had a tour group arriving the next day.

I found myself rattling around alone in the empty, echoing, barn-like dining room that had once been the station cafeteria. There were wooden tables and chairs, hefty rafters overhead, wooden pillars down the centre, and a worn but lovely parquet floor. All along one wall, waist-high windows opened onto the platform, where passengers used to line up to buy refreshments. Long tables covered in white cloth took up the middle of the massive room, while an open fireplace fronted by armchairs filled one end and a substantial wooden bar extended almost the entire width of it at the other. You don't see bars like that any more. On it was arranged an assortment of whisky jugs and trade figurines, including a pair of Black and White Whisky Scotty dogs and a White Horse figurine that would have gladdened the heart of any collector.

This place brought happy memories of the railway refreshment rooms of Balaclava, South Australia, a stopping place for the trains I had travelled on during my childhood.

Behind the bar, a wide wooden staircase ascended to rooms that had once served train passengers who stayed overnight. Previous guests of this hotel read like a list of the world's wildlife luminaries and include David Attenborough and my favourite, Gerald Durrell, whose *My Family and Other Animals* is still the funniest book I have ever read.

I would have loved to sleep in this old building, but now those rooms were closed and the accommodation was across the road in a row of A-framed, chalet-style cabins snuggled against a tree-covered mountain. I entered my chalet and found it had been built entirely of local produce, mostly wood and rattan. The thatched roof sloped down to touch the side of the bed and although the room was teeny inside, the roof rose to a great peak. The plank floor waved up and down like the deck of a ship at sea when I walked across it to the minuscule bathroom, which had been tacked on the back. There were no fly screens and no glass in the window, so I was pleased to see mosquito netting draped across the rickety wooden bed. The entry door opened onto a small porch, on which I could sit and watch people walk to and from the nearby village of Andasabe.

One part of the chalet's construction puzzled me. It had a back door that opened onto the toilet. You were hardly likely to be admitting guests through the loo, though I suppose it could come in handy for ejecting an admirer if your husband came home unexpectedly.

Later, lunching in majestic solitude in the cavernous railway buffet dining room, I mused that they must have done a big trade here in the station's heyday, while under French administration. Perhaps those days might return. I was thrilled when a goods train pulled into the station right beside me. It stood, still panting from its exertions, where I could admire the entire length of it through the windows that opened onto the platform. Then, with the greatest possible noise, excitement and commotion, workers began to unload the train.

On the platform I found the stationmaster. He told me the line was just now being reopened, and there would be one freight and one passenger train a week between Moramanga and Brickaville.

Intent on exploring the village of Andasibe, described in my guidebook as a sleepy former logging village, I followed the rutted dirt track that led to it. The path crossed the road and the railway line, meandered among bushes and trees, dipped to a bridge over a pretty river, then entered the village on the river's opposite bank. I appeared to be a great novelty in this humble village. A mere line of ramshackle wooden houses, a couple of stone buildings and a post office, it attracts few travellers. But it boasts two churches, both big affairs with tall spires. One Protestant, one Catholic, from higher ground on opposite sides, they dominate the village.

Returning from my walk, on the road I met the Gare hotel's manager, an amiable individual immaculately dressed in a white suit and carrying a large black umbrella. Speaking English like the gentry, he asked me if I had found accommodation for the following day yet, then added, 'Do not worry, if you do not acquire a room I shall arrange something for you.'

The only other hotel in the vicinity was the Feon'ny Ala, three kilometres down the road. I asked the waiter at the Gare if I could use the phone to reserve a room there. He told me the phone was broken. I spied a phone box outside on the side of the road and asked him if that worked. He conferred with his mate and they agreed that, yes, it did. Of course, it didn't. I would have to go to the Feon'ny Ala in person. The only way to do this, I was told, was to hail a *taxi brousse* as one travelled past, but they were rare at this time of the day.

There was nothing for it but to walk the six kilometres there and back. It took me two hours, and I was escorted almost all the way by a dozen or more children, all chewing sticks of raw sugar cane, on their way home from school. They formed a Brat Pack Inspection Squad, taking turns to march beside me in order to have a close-up scrutiny of my strangeness. My hair, skin and clothes received rapt and minute examination and a running commentary was passed back to those behind and discussed in detail. I showed them the guidebook I was carrying and they oo'ed and ah'ed excitedly over the pictures of the animals they recognised. At around the three-kilometre mark the children dropped off to take a track that seemed to lead nowhere but into the oblivion of the forest. Goodness knows how much further they had to go, and barefooted at that.

The Feon'ny Ala, a collection of small chalet huts, sat surrounded by flowers and gardens right on the edge of the forest of the national park. Peace is easy to find in Madagascar, I had discovered. The woman in charge promised me a room for the next day, and I walked back to Andasibe, tailed for a while by a couple of teenage lads until they said respectfully, 'Au revoir, Madame' and turned off up a sidetrack and disappeared among the trees.

Then I was alone to enjoy the forest. The road traverses the Parc National de Mantadia and its edges were covered with dense vegetation, which was so thick I couldn't see much further than a couple of metres in. Onto the road spilled ferns, vines, yellow and red flowering bushes of lantana, mauve love-in-the-mist, a bush with a white trumpet-shaped bloom, yellow nasturtiums, and other red, purple and yellow flowers that were unfamiliar to me. Sweet perfume wafted out from a sun-drenched hollow filled with pink roses. Behind the undergrowth bigger ferns and bushes rose, then came the trees, large and small, from which a myriad of birds called.

Suddenly I heard a chilling sound, the roaring of an animal that sounded like a lion. It came again, menacing and primeval, breaking through the tranquillity of the surrounding forest. I continued walking and when I came to the gatehouse of the national park I asked the guard what had made the cry. He said it was the fossa, or the Malagasy civet, a small carnivore about the size of a domestic cat. This is not to be confused with the fosa, Madagascar's largest carnivore.

That night I lost my majestic solitude dining status in the Gare. A French group arrived for dinner and a few local people wandered in to sit at the bar. I watched the tour guide harangue his flock of captives then shepherd them out, and while I envied their minibus, I wouldn't have wanted to join them.

My zebu steak came replete with a cerise bougainvillea flower artfully surrounded by tiny ferns. The Malagasy have soul, I decided.

Andasibe was much colder than Tana. I slept under two blankets, wearing most of my clothes, but it was worth it to wake in the morning surrounded by the sounds of the forest. Fine rain accompanied me across the road to breakfast, but it soon stopped and I knew I had to move on to my accommodation for this night. Sure that someone would help me, I didn't worry how this would come about: Madagascar's fatalism is infectious.

Discovering that the phones were working now I tried again to contact the outside world. It was still there! My ever-loving nephew told me cheerfully that my house had burned down and the cat had been abducted by aliens. With relatives like him I don't need enemies.

Another infusion of black coffee and I was ready to face the move. A *taxi brousse* soon came along in the shape of a utility with a canvas cover. The driver dropped the tailgate, heaved me over it and shoved me inside. I crashed along to a space on the bench at the far end, falling on knees and tripping over bundles and the spare wheel on the floor. Many hands reached out to steady me and help me along, and with *excuse mois* and *pardons*, I made the safety of the vacant spot and plonked on the wooden bench next to a woman breastfeeding a tiny baby. Passengers don't shift for you because the last one got the worst seat, and one furthest from the flap.

'*Salama*,' I said all round when I had restored my equilibrium.

'*Vous eetaleean?*' I was asked, and when we had established that I was of a species that they seemed to consider even more exotic than the Italian, we spent the rest of the time it took to reach my destination getting acquainted.

At the gates of the Hotel Feon'ny Ala I scrambled out, followed by a chorus of *au revoirs* and *bon voyages* and forked out the twenty cents the ride had cost.

My fabulous new home was a chalet in touching distance of the forest. As I arrived, the *indri* were calling. These arboreal creatures are the largest lemur and grow to about ninety centimetres. Like Superman, they are able to leap tall buildings in a single bound – well, ten metres between trees actually. Their Malagasy name is *babakoto*, which means 'the song of the forest'. Song was not quite the word I would have used. It was more like Pavarotti competing with an ambulance siren – their rowdy yodelling can be heard up to three kilometres away! The *indris* called until after eleven in the morning this day and although it was quite an experience to hear them, I never got to see one. Few people do. You have to be up and out in the forest extremely early to do so I was told. This, and the fact that I had to leave then anyway, convinced me that the song I heard and the photos I saw were enough. Different in appearance to other types of lemur, *indris* have teddy bear ears that make them look whimsical and cuddly.

The bed in my little house was perched on a platform, reached by a wooden ladder, and faced a glass-less window through which the forest foliage gently inserted a leaf or two. I slept with the trees. The word 'paradise' sprang to mind. A calm river, set deep in a narrow, green-clad gully beneath, separated me from the forest. I could step onto a balcony that hung over the ravine above the river and, leaning out, stroke the branches of the big trees that spanned the gap.

Deciding on a foray of discovery straight away after check-in,

I climbed down the path that wound its way along the river, among white arum lilies, shocking pink impatiens, and brilliant red day lilies, to enter the forest. Here the vegetation was dark and looped with lianas. Small streams trickled between moss-covered boulders. Under the roof, formed by the highest trees, grew bamboos, palms, tree ferns and orchids. No sound came to me except the honk of frogs and birdcalls.

The place to eat during the day was looking over the river on the Feon'ny Ala's wide balcony. Over lunch that day one of the friendly staff and I plotted an afternoon adventure. Marco agreed to help me hire the hotel's car – the only one in the district – to take me to the Vacona Lodge Resort and Reserve. I had no use for the Resort, an upmarket haunt of French tour groups, but it came with the Reserve, the place where, I was assured, I could get up close and personal with lemurs – an idea that excited me no end. Though how the lemurs felt about it I didn't know.

We set off in a four-wheel drive Nissan, the most upmarket vehicle I had come in contact with so far in Madagascar. The 4WD part of it proved to be very necessary. Vacona was only fifteen kilometres away but the twisting dirt track that ran among the soaring mountains was rutted and holed. We bumped through Andasibe village; passing the two grandiose churches, I grumbled to myself it was a pity they couldn't have used the money to build a road instead. Up, up, we drove, ever higher, until we arrived at the Lodge behind its boom gates.

This lovely resort features a reception desk and restaurant sitting in the middle of a lake, which are accessed by a quaint wooden bridge. Guests stay in chalets, rather beyond my budget, on the slopes that rise from the central lake area.

Marco informed me that Vacona is the name of the rattan the Malagasy use to build houses and everything else imaginable. Then he went off to siesta under a tree. A local guide, Renna, assumed custody of me, tramping me off to see the animals. We hiked a long distance, along tracks and paths hemmed by forest, until we reached a small, enclosed lake where forty-five big crocodiles lived. I could have gladly given this malevolent-looking lot a miss. Renna told me they were fed on Saturdays. It was only Friday, but they were already lying about in wait. As we wobbled across the lake above them on a gyrating rope bridge, I hoped that they were not about to receive a bonus appetiser.

We hiked on to an enclosure housing the animal whose bloodcurdling howls I had heard along the edge of the forest the day before. The male fossa, almost a metre long, rather resembled the photos I have seen of the Tasmanian tiger. The smaller female had recently produced two babies, but dad, unimpressed, had eaten them for dinner.

Elsewhere, Renna encouraged me to cuddle a male boa constrictor, and I wrapped all two-and-a-half metres of its muscly strength around my neck for just long enough to have my photo taken. This was indeed a beautiful creature, and its black and white skin felt warm and smooth. His mate, the brown female, Renna told me, was antisocial. I wasn't about to try to prove him wrong.

Birds flew around us and an occasional tortoise ambled across the path like a geriatric who'd lost his walking frame. Eventually we reached the far side of the lake where the lemurs lived on an island sanctuary. We climbed into a canoe and Renna paddled me across.

Three different species of lemur lived on this island, the brown, the ruffed, and the grey. The ones I saw had bodies around sixty centimetres or so in length with a tail as long again. They were very tame – as I walked among the trees holding out banana and carrot pieces, they swung down leisurely one at a time to my level. Then, holding the tree with one paw, they would gently put the other out to take my offering. Every now and then a more daring one dropped softly onto my shoulder. As the lemurs touched me with their velvety paws that were almost hands, I was astounded at the delicacy with which they used them. I had expected the boisterousness of monkeys, but lemurs are far too well mannered to pull off your hat and tug at your hairdo.

They were so handsome – and they seemed to know it. One white and black ruffed lemur, in particular, adopted a photogenic stance whenever I pointed my camera at him. He knew he was gorgeous and behaved like a pro. Paris Hilton eat your heart out: he didn't stand pigeon-toed and knock-kneed!

One brown lemur mother had a five-day-old baby, so small I could have held him comfortably in one of my hands. He clung for dear life to his mum's furry side as she swung nonchalantly from branch to branch. She descended to take a banana from my hand, allowing me to admire her offspring close-up.

I spent a blissful couple of hours wandering along the island's small dirt paths through the forest and encountered many more lemurs. Some approached hopeful that I might be a source of snacks, others seemed just curious and came to inspect, and sometimes touch, me. It was an unforgettable experience.

Toward sunset Renna and I meandered back across the water to find Marco, and we returned to the Feon'ny Ala.

The next day I was due to meet Madabus to venture on to Toamasina, but encountered much confusion as to where the bus would stop. The opinion at the Feon'ny Ala was that it called there. But staff at the information centre at the park entrance thought they owned the spot, as did the manager of the Gare. I opted for the middle course. That was where the bus had stopped first when I had arrived in Andasibe.

The morning dawned late, freezing and misty, but a steaming hot shower soon fixed that. After heaps of coffee I discovered that the only car the hotel possessed, and which I needed to take me to the park centre two kilometres away, was gone. I wasn't about to walk that road, dragging my bag behind me. One of the obliging hotel staff took me down to a spot on the road where he said I would be able to hail a passing *taxi brousse*. He carried my bag to a roadside hut and told the owners, who sat in front of it on rattan mats on the grass, what to do with me. I attempted to sit down on the ground with them, but they said, 'No no!' and produced a miniscule stool. There I squatted enjoying the sunshine with several smiling women and the usual brood of babies, one of whom immediately crawled over to investigate my shoelaces, objects that I had noticed were a novelty in this community of bare feet or sandals.

Time went by. I heard pigs squealing with joy behind the wooden paling fence and presumed it was feeding time, but still no vehicle appeared on the empty road. At last a 4WD came in sight and I leapt up to hail it, thinking it was the hotel car returning. Only after I had installed myself and we were on our way did I discover that the young man driving it had nothing to do with the hotel. He was a private tour operator just passing through to collect a French group at the Vacona Lodge, but he cheerfully drove me to the rendezvous with Madabus.

17 In Search of Pirate Treasure

Leaving Andasibe, I was now on my way to the coast, first to Toamasina and from there to Ile Saint Marie, a diving and whale-watching destination. But that was not why I wanted to visit this island. It is also the site of legendary pirate treasure.

The Madabus driver flung the bus along the road to Toamasina as fast as was humanly possible, but I had deliberately taken a seat way up the back where I couldn't see danger staring me in the face. What the eye doesn't see the heart doesn't grieve on. For a couple of hours the road undulated like a serpent's back. The bus swept up and down mountains and swung around elbow bends, throwing me from side to side. We passed a truck that had failed to make a bend – the sight of its wreckage sprinkled down the mountainside made me feel ill. Men were attempting salvage operations, hauling goods up by ropes over the edge of the precipice, under which the ground fell away abruptly into the void.

Later in our journey, the forest thinned and here and there the hillsides were scarred with bare patches where slash and burn operations had been carried out. As we approached the coast and Brickaville – a no-horse town if ever I saw one – large plantations of sugar cane lined the road. Close to the coast ran a French-built waterway, the Canal de Pangalanes, created by cutting links for 600 kilometres between rivers and lakes to form a navigable route to the port of Toamasina in the north.

The bus had to wait an hour in Brickaville to collect any

passengers who might come from the canals. I supported local enterprise by purchasing a large hand of bananas from a woman at a roadside shack. No canal travellers appeared and we resumed our journey. After Brickaville we drove parallel with the coast through country that was mostly flat, crossing many bridges that spanned the canal.

Finally, five-and-a-half hours later, we approached Toamasina and, after a rough ride over the appalling streets of the outskirts, we were unloaded in the town centre. My map showed that the hotel I had managed to book ahead by phone, the Generation, was in the main street just around the corner from where Madabus had stopped. I took a *pousse pousse* to it. Here they were a different breed of rickshaw, with penny-farthing wheels and brightly coloured bodies that made them resemble old-fashioned babies' prams.

'Ah,' said the young man at the hotel when I arrived. 'I was waiting for you. The lady with the nice name and the nice voice.' Masterfully hiding his disappointment, he smiled at me. He had been expecting someone young and beautiful, but what clattered in the door under a fright wig, clutching bananas, was a frowsy old bat in a decidedly tatty state.

After cleaning myself up a little, I walked out to view the town and decided that I liked Toamasina. It has wide streets that are easy to navigate and it is a genuine port. I find something exotic about towns that engage in the commerce of the sea. From the main street, which is only one back from the sea, I could see lines of big ships docked along the waterfront. In colonial times Toamasina was a resort as well as Madagascar's principal port. The other major street is an attractive, tree-lined boulevard with a garden down its centre. It crosses the main street, running from the now defunct train station to the harbour. I strolled about exploring until well after dark but felt quite safe. The guidebook had labelled Toamasina a dreary, uninteresting town, but I found that every time this book's writers bagged a place, I thought the opposite. They and I marched to a different drum, their tastes leaning heavily toward surf and sand.

The Generation Hotel was a bit strange in that my bathroom was right in the room with me. The shower lurked behind a curtain in one corner and the toilet did the same on the other side. Another curtain could be drawn across in front of the pair of them to segregate the rest of the room. From the balcony I looked down into the main street and saw colonial-style buildings and walls heavily stained with the black mould of the tropics. The houses, with their spacious, open verandas surrounded by columns, were different from the houses I had seen in Tana and Antsirabe.

The Generation, I was to discover, turned into an echo chamber at night. It had large, open, tiled expanses of floor between the rooms, as well as wide stairways and a battalion of noisy male guests. I did not sleep well and awoke grumpy when the alarm shrilled in the predawn light, reminding me that I had to get up to catch a bus.

In a *pousse pousse*, sealed by heavy plastic and whose driver I had to pay double as was the custom when it was raining, I was launched into a tropical downpour. I couldn't see anything from inside this mobile tomb and he could have been taking me anywhere, but I hoped I would make it to the bus before it left.

Emerging once more into the land of the living, I found myself in a muddy side street where the minibus for Ivongo, the coastal village that was the launching pad for boats to Ile St Marie, stood waiting. In the office I joined an assortment of travellers fortifying themselves with the strong coffee the bus company had provided. There was even cake – at six in the morning! I hopped in.

I was greeted by three French boys I had met previously on the bus from Andasibe to Brickaville. They were in a sorry state, although one looked happy about it (he was the one who had gone missing with a girl). The other two had spent the night looking for him, panic-stricken, thinking him dead in a ditch with his throat cut. He had sloped off in the early hours of the morning from the dive where they had been partying, but had failed to tell his friends that he was leaving. They all looked frazzled and when we got on the bus they curled up in a tangled heap like puppies and fell asleep.

The rain cleared as we headed up the coast. There were mountains, but they were not as high as in the centre of the country. They were covered with the same dense vegetation, interspersed with areas under cultivation. We had to ford countless waterways as we crossed the paths of all the rivers and streams of the interior that flow down here on their way to the sea. We clattered and clanged over one big metal pontoon and many bridges. The promised one-hour bus ride metamorphosed into a three-hour marathon. I was not surprised, and it gave me a chance to sleep. Getting up at five in the morning is not a breeze for someone who considers nine the crack of dawn.

Our destination, Ile St Marie, is a small, skinny island off Madagascar's east coast and measures fifty-seven kilometres long and eight kilometres wide. French settlers tried to form a colony here in the 1640s, but were beaten by tropical fevers, predominantly cerebral malaria, which killed most of them. This got very bad press, but it did create the island's main defence against European colonial invasion. Later that century Ile St Marie became the hideout of a miscellaneous collection of villains – English, French, American, and Portuguese – whose chief line of work was piracy. From Ile St Marie they preyed upon ships, passing en route to and from India and from the Cape of Good Hope to Europe and the Far East, carrying lucrative loot.

A tougher breed than the good-living settlers, many of these sea wolves outwitted the fevers, married the local women, and their progeny thrived. By 1700 Ile St Marie was the pirate capital of the world and at one stage was home to a thousand nefarious inhabitants.

Ivongo, the tiny seaside village from where boats make the voyage to Ile St Marie, has capitalised on the long delays for a sea-crossing by providing a basic eating place. I ordered coffee and an omelette and had a splash in their squat toilet out the back. A ginger cat was languidly brushed off the table, where it had been comfortably curled, to make room for my plate; he joined the three other cats who romped up to compete with me for my food. Ever a softie when it comes to an entreating meow, I gave them some of my baguette.

After my meal I joined a line of local people roosting on a wooden bench beside the water, waiting for the boat. A mother goose waddled imperiously along between our feet, honking to her one downy gosling each time it strayed.

The major reason for the delay here was that all passengers had to register with the police at the nearby checkpoint before being allowed to board the boat. The ferry that previously had made the crossing sank in 2000 and many people, including tourists, were drowned. As it is bad for business to kill off the patrons, controls were now considered necessary. It didn't make the voyage any safer, I imagine, but at least there was a record of who ended up feeding the fishes.

The trip is now made in a small speedboat. We were ticked off the police list as we boarded, then made to put on life jackets before the boat could leave the shore. Not a great morale-booster, especially as I was thinking about the sharks that frequented these waters. I was sure they were out there waiting for me.

As I sat patiently in the boat I wondered what all the fuss was about. There was the island, straight ahead across a short stretch of calm water, clearly visible from land. Right? Wrong! That was merely the other side of the lagoon. This tranquil water I saw before me was only the beginning of our journey. We had to traverse a stretch of open sea, and to reach that we had to pass through a channel where the boat was pitched and tossed alarmingly. And this was on a fine day – it must be pretty bad on a rough one. Once the channel had been safely negotiated, the sea was choppy but no longer violent.

The boat's bench seats were hard and narrow, arranged in tight rows. Two fat French ladies squashed in alongside me, pushing me hard against a Malagasy girl on the other side. What was it with two fat ladies and me? Now I had found another pair. Oh well, they made a good wind and spray shield. As soon as the danger of capsizing in the channel had passed, the Malagasy girl relaxed and fell sound asleep with her head on my shoulder.

Two hours later we reached Ambodifotatra, the Ile's only town. I strolled into the cafe on the landing and asked about accommodation. Knowing there would be someone nearby touting rooms, I was happy to allow myself to be touted upon. In the past I have found some great places this way rather than using the guidebook's recommendations. Soon a young man appeared who convinced me that he had a hotel just perfect for me.

He bumped my bag along the unpaved dusty main street on the seafront until we came to a small two-storeyed hotel. The Hortensia *was* just what I wanted – the entrance was in the street, while at the back, the rooms fronted the sea, separated only by a ribbon of lawn edged by a retaining wall on which the waves lapped.

My room on the top floor had double glass doors that led out onto a wide veranda overlooking the sea. I could survey the entire bay and the coast all the way around to the boat landing. Further on I could make out the palace of Queen Bety, once ruler of the island. Beyond, was a tiny peaked island that rose from the sea, alone like a pimple on a pumpkin. One solitary tree sat atop its peak waving like a flag. When I asked about the island I was told that nobody went there – it is *fady* to do so.

In the days I spent in this sublime spot I was able to watch the tide coming and going under the coconut palms that leaned out from the shore. Fishermen passed by in their canoes. I could even see the sea from my bed, a mosquito net-surrounded, four-poster that dominated the large room. A bed like this, with four convenient posts, was an admirable way to mosquito-proof yourself. I imagine in Europe the posts were hung with draperies to keep the cold air from sleepers in draughty castles, but the beds had adapted well to the tropics and their antique looks suited the seventeenth-century ambience of this island. Sleeping inside a mosquito-net tent in a four-poster bed, with waves foaming on the shore directly beneath, is blissful.

At five o'clock of my first day I surfaced from my siesta to go for a walk in the cool breeze blowing in from the sea. Up and down the town I ambled, enjoying everything except the difficulty of walking on the broken surface of the road. Ambo is a very small place, mostly dotted along the one wide, unpaved road. The columned verandas of the buildings gave the town a colonial feel. There were a few microscopic shops, mainly offering craft items for tourists, but this was no tourist haunt. Most tourists went straight to the beach hotels that spread down the coast. I had the town to myself.

Wonderfully fine rattan goods dominated the craft shops and I invested in a tremendous hat – large and pink to match my umbrella – for the ridiculous price of two dollars. The evening market was just setting up crude wooden stalls behind the main, and only, street. A roadside cafe provided me with dinner, and I provided a meal for the local insects, which were legion. The food was slightly dearer than on the mainland but it was good.

A hideously noisy generator by the boat landing supplied the town's electricity. The din it made could be heard all over town all day, but thankfully it stopped at night. Even before its official time of retirement, it frequently packed up and left the town in pitch dark. I had to stumble home during one of these time-outs, but once there I looked out from my balcony over a sea lit by an almost full moon and watched the bobbing lanterns of people wading along the shore gathering seafood.

I was woken at five the next morning by a heavy downpour, which cleansed the day and made it beautiful. It was so good to be back in the tropics. Hard to believe that two nights ago I had been really cold and sleeping in all my clothes. A five-hour bus ride had taken me from the chill of the mountains to the warmth of the coast. I lay in bed luxuriating in comfort until children's voices rose from the beach. Leaning over the balcony I watched them turning over rocks and looking underneath for the tiny crabs to use as bait. A small naked boy paddled among them on a piece of board and from the property next door a man pushed out a canoe. Then more sounds arose from the town and across from the boat landing the throb of the generator started again. The town was getting up and it was time I did too.

Breakfast was served on the downstairs veranda within spitting reach of the sea. I was alone until I asked the woman proprietor if she knew of a way I could get to the buccaneer's cemetery, located beside the Baie des Forbans (Pirate's Bay). In a short time she conjured up Henrie, who spoke some English, and I signed him on as my guide. We set off in a car with a driver Henrie had enlisted.

The major star in the island's past was that well-known scoundrel, Captain William Kidd, a Scotsman who had been the boss cocky here for some time. Finally captured by the English, he was taken back to Britain and interrogated as to the whereabouts of his legendary fabulous treasure. He did not oblige, so they hung him in a fit of pique. Big mistake – they are still looking for his ill-gotten gains. The whereabouts of his ship, the *Adventure*, which had been sunk off the coast, was known, but the treasure was not in her. She still lies at the entrance to Ile aux Forbans. Since then many fortune hunters have come looking. There is no doubt that the treasure exists, but where? I for one would dearly like to know. Rumours abound, and many are focused around a cave at the far end of the island.

Henrie, the driver and I set off through the town. We passed the oldest Catholic church in Madagascar. An 1857 gift from the French Empress Eugenie, it stands on a high point overlooking the sea. Crossing a causeway built of rocks, we came to the former palace of the local queen, Bety, who married a French ex-army officer. Bety was the daughter of King Ratsimilaho – the son of an English pirate – and she rescued the dubious fellow she later married, who had been cast adrift for misbehaving with a fellow officer's wife in Reunion. He obviously had a way with women and Bety was no exception. Under his influence, Queen Bety ceded Ile St Marie to France in 1750. Two years later a revolt erupted, French settlers were massacred, and poor old Bety was shunted off into exile. In 1818 the French returned and got even by turning the island into a penal colony. When independence arrived for Madagascar in 1960, the island, understandably, voted to renounce French nationality and join the Malagasy Republic.

I thought Bety's place more colonial mansion than palace, but its position, looking into the bay, was peerless.

Access to the other side of the bay and the cemetery was achieved by crossing another causeway further on. This one was so narrow that only one car at a time could take it on. It was Sunday and small boys were fishing from the causeway edges. On the other side we stopped beside a couple of village houses from where Henrie and I had a half-hour's walk on an isolated foot track through dim, coconut-palm-shaded paths of dark sand and grass. The sides of the path were pocked by holes, the homes of scuttling land crabs. Henrie told me that, although they make good food, *fady* prohibits the eating of them – which explains why there are so many of the blighters.

Henrie was walking proof that there is little dental care in Madagascar. He was only about forty, but he had no teeth at all. Perhaps because of this, he felt the need to spit often. Walking behind and downwind, I soon learned to take evasive action when I heard a missile coming.

The path to the cemetery dips to the tidal flats and crosses creeks, the first by means of a slippery, thirty-centimetre wide piece of rusty metal. Henrie held my hand and hauled me across. We made our way over causeways of old metal girders, long lines of slimy rocks, and skinny logs. In between I sloshed along in water up to my ankles, my shoes thoroughly soaked. I'd forgotten how good it is to splash in puddles.

Henrie brought me back to reality by reminding me that if I dallied here for too long the tide would cut us off. Land access to the island is only possible at low tide. Otherwise you need to come by boat, as the pirates would have done. The causeways were built only recently. Charming place to spend the night, I thought, a haunted cemetery chockas with the ghosts of the worst possible kind of villain.

Reaching the top of this high, narrow spit of land I was in the cemetery, a shaded, spooky place. To be buried in the Pirate's Cemetery had entailed a last ride in a boat, which struck me as very fitting for a seafarer. But not only pirates are buried here. I found the graves of their wives and children and of corsairs, who were pirates with a degree of legitimacy. They did not freelance; they worked for the local king. As well as renegade Europeans, there were local pirates, some risen from the ranks of slaves the pirates had bought from the island's king to work on their ships. Reading the dates on the tombstones I could see that life expectancy here had not been high. Apart from the fevers of this unhealthy climate, 'Occupation: Pirate' would not read well to a life-insurance assessor.

A large tombstone stood in the centre of the graveyard. It had Captain Kidd's name on it, but he was not here. Other pirates, who revered him, erected it as a memorial after the British had unsportingly hung him.

There was also a large grave with an inscription dedicated to 'The Unknown Pirate'. It was decorated with a crudely carved skull and crossbones. Another grave belonged to one Captain Thomas, no pirate, but a perfectly respectable English gent who was buried here in 1875. Henrie said his family comes every five years to tend his grave.

From this spot, high up, I could see across to the Catholic Church on the other side of the Baie des Forbans and to the Ile aux Forbans, the small island in the centre where the pirates had lived. The bay is almost circular, with a narrow entrance that hides the wide area inside from the Indian Ocean, where ships laden with cargo had passed by. It was a perfect spot to lie in wait, sail out, pounce on unsuspecting ships, steal their goods, and retreat to safety. Sadly nothing remains of the pirates' wooden houses. Cyclones hit this island regularly and they have all been blown away.

Back in the town for lunch I met another cat, a big tabby tom who begged for his share. I grappled with the menu until Madame, the proprietor, called a lady on the phone who asked me what I wanted. I said fish, any sort, anyhow. By the time it came an hour later, tabby and I were calling piteously for sustenance, but it was worth waiting for.

I spent a couple more days on Ile St Marie enjoying a quiet life beside the sea and watching the coming and going at the dock and the town. Early on my last morning I went looking for the post office. Even at that time it was steamy walking in the sun and I got sweaty and lost. The post office was not in the main street, but way above the town looking out to sea.

Just as well there was a full moon that night, as the generator went on strike for three hours. I had to pack by two-candle power. Then it was another up-at-five morning to catch the boat back to the mainland at six. By now I was beginning to get the hang of this early rising – but I just don't want that information to get about and have it expected of me in the future. All you have to do to rise up singing in the misty pre-dawn is go to bed with the fowls. Cuts out partying-on though.

The boat left on time, and once again we seafarers were ticked off the list as we clambered aboard. Twenty passengers crammed into the launch. There were no fat ladies among them, but I wished there were. It was colder and rougher and there was more sea spray. A Malagasy woman next to me was seasick for the entire two-hour ride. The sick bags were, unfortunately, clear plastic, giving me a close-up view of the former contents of her stomach. She had an extraordinary amount in there for someone who might have known she would lose them.

The sea was pounding in great rollers as we came to the channel entrance, and the boat driver looked over his shoulder constantly. Was he trying to surf in on the waves? It seemed so. As we cut across the breakers at an angle, it felt as though the launch would tip over, but we made it safely to the calmness of the lagoon.

On the landing a young man handed out our baggage. 'You are alone?' he asked me. I nodded. 'Okay, I will take care of you.' He carried my bag all the way to the bus and took my passport to register my safe return with the police. He was one of the few fluent English-speakers I had found in the country so I gave him my copy of *'Tis*. You'd have thought I'd given him a gold mine! Perhaps I did. Maybe he discovered the meaning of life in St John.

There was a long wait for the bus to leave so I sat in the eating place and had coffee with Madame. The police came personally to return my passport to me. Five-star stuff, no standing in line at the post for me. Here in Ivongo the police took the shape of a good-looking young woman and man, both in smart white shirts, dark-blue pants and grey berets.

Eventually the bus departed and we were back in Toamasina by lunchtime. Deciding to try another hotel, I took a *pousse pousse* to the Hotel Flamboyant, and was shown to a decent room that was even cheaper than the Generation. I hoped it might be also quieter. The management must have had connections in the fake-flower trade – vases, pots, troughs, tubs, and trees of these insults to mother nature assaulted my eyesight wherever I looked.

Intent on lunch, I passed by their attractive dining room and chose a chair at the pavement cafe. But after being set upon by a determined bunch of vendors flapping tablecloths at me, I beat a hasty retreat back into the dining room. I use these trappings of civilisation only occasionally and the idea of stuffing my bag with them to lump around the country was ludicrous. (I had my wooden condiment set to consider.) The hustlers outside refused to see the logic in this, however, and continued to wave semaphore messages at me through the dining-room windows.

I had arranged for the same *pousse pousse* man to return and take me to the market. I still owed him the previous fare, as I'd had no change before. I didn't have to go looking for him, he was at the door, determined not to let me out of his sight.

The market was big and interesting, with clothes, rattan ware, woodcarvings and some tourist stuff. I strolled back along the attractive cornice lined with seats and gardens, palms and big trees. A flotilla of cargo boats was anchored along the sea edge. In a phone box I successfully phoned to reserve a bed in the guesthouse on Lac Ampitabe, down the

Canal de Pangalanes, my next destination. And in a side street I came upon a small supermarket where I bought emergency rations – water, yoghurt, cheese and peanuts. I passed on the *Gouty* biscuits though.

18 Cruising the Canal

I was woken at five in the morning by a torrential downpour drumming on the roof of the Flamboyant – just what you don't want to hear when you are about to spend several hours in an open boat. But the rain had cleared by the time I left. I set off early, which turned out to be a good idea, as the boat proved almost impossible to find. The taxi the hotel receptionist had found for me bumped along the mud tracks, splashed through a gateway, and entered a large yard filled with trucks and shipping containers, behind which a few old boats skulked below the high bank of a muddy river. Was this the Port Fluvial, the major river port? A more dismal site would be hard to find. I could see nothing remotely resembling the launch I had been told left from here for the trip down the Canal de Pangales to my destination at Lac Ampitabe.

Sure that we had come to the wrong place, I convinced the taxidriver to go back into the street and try again. But there was no other entrance to the river nearby. Then I saw the mobile phone on the taxi's dashboard. I implored the driver to phone the contact number I had been given for the boat company. With fresh directions we returned to the alleged Port Fluvial, but still could not see the boat. The driver phoned again and then, down some steps below eye level, we located the previously invisible launch. It waited, deserted, and with no sign to give a clue to its identity. Just then, however, the boatman arrived, lugging two petrol drums. He and I waited a while, but no one else came, so we chugged off alone.

The small outboard motorboat was open, except for an overhead canvas canopy, and it was windy and cold out on the river. Then it rained. The driver wrapped me in a cocoon of green stuff that looked like old garbage bags (unused, I hoped); I had achieved plastification! Despite the promises made for this beauty treatment I had seen advertised in Tana, it didn't improve me one bit.

At first we travelled down a wide river, passing wooden canoes, rafts made of green bamboo, and now and then a passenger boat – small, rough-looking wooden craft riding low in the water, crammed with people. The ladies called '*bon jour!*' to me and the kids all waved. We passed an occasional village, zoomed once under a railway bridge, and manoeuvred around the many fish traps, which marched from the bank out into the middle of the river, leaving only a narrow opening for boats to slot through. The traps, constructed of bamboo poles stuck into the riverbed, formed zigzags that the fish entered and, not being very intelligent, couldn't fathom how to get out of again.

Some of the canoes I saw were paddled along, others propelled by poles. Many were piled with coconuts, bananas and vegetables and were heading for the market in Toamasina. Some others had, to my sorrow, heaps of freshly cut trees, more evidence of the stripping of the forest which causes erosion, a major problem in Madagascar. Everywhere I went along the East Coast I saw piles of wood for sale.

Later we came to less populated areas where the forest grew right down to the water's edge. We cruised past riverbanks covered with creepers, ferns and palms. Now and then I saw women washing clothes on small sandy beaches where small *pirogues* – wooden canoes – were pulled up under trees.

After several hours I reached my destination, the Bush Haus, a guesthouse in a lonely spot on the shore of Lac Ampitabe, close to the nature reserve I wanted to visit. I was dropped off at the end of a very long wooden jetty – necessary due to the shallowness of the lake – from where the manager, a friendly Frenchman, escorted me ashore. He introduced me to his Malagasy wife and his mother-in-law – 'the grandmere of my babee' – and his gorgeous, chubby little girl. The stiff breeze on the river had been chilling, but a good breakfast in the dining area, high above the lake and open on three sides to views of water and woods, resuscitated me.

The Bush Haus was a simple place but it had style. The fruit on the breakfast table was beautifully arranged in a miniature wooden canoe. Elevated from the lakeside, the accommodation consisted of huts dotted up and down the small hills surrounding the al fresco dining and sitting area. Each self-contained hut was made of wood, with a rattan interior and a thatched roof, and was fronted by a wide veranda looking out to the forest on one side and the lake on the other.

In the dining room I met again the German students from the bus to Andasibe. They were camping in the forest at the back of the Bush Haus in order to study the more than sixty species of pitcher plants – especially a giant form that is found nowhere else in the world – that grow on a nearby islet, the Ile aux Nepenthes (Island of Pitcher Plants). These cunning carnivores produce enticing nectar – the poor innocent insect that thinks he has popped in for a snack, soon finds, to his disgust, that he is the main item on the menu. The students were hoping to publish a thesis on the subject.

After lunch I set off to walk two kilometres around the beach to the reserve, le Reserve d'akanin'ny Nofy (for short). The beach was a narrow strip of white sand fringed by dense forest that ran down to it, sometimes from sharply rising hillsides. In many places trickling streams tinkled down from the forested hills above, meandering across the sand over beds of multicoloured stones their waters had brought from the interior. The walk along the beach was a rock hound's delight. I picked up a few of the stones, putting a diamond or two in my pocket – I wish.

The only sign of life among the thick vegetation were a couple of rattan houses. At one stage I had to wade across the river where it entered the lake. Fortunately its width narrowed as it reached the shore and the water was only knee-deep. The manager had warned me about the river before I left the Bush Haus and I had ascertained that it wasn't tidal. I didn't want to have to swim on the way back, crocodiles and sharks featuring largely in my visions of this feat.

A wooden jetty and a long flight of steps ascending the hillside marked the entrance to the reserve. Climbing to an outdoor bar and office, I located a young man who agreed to be my guide. We wandered through the forest for two hours and I saw five kinds of lemur, including a hybrid produced from two species that had intermarried, a rare thing in mammals. One of the latter accidentally bit me when I offered him a banana. I let out a squeak and the lemur looked deeply embarrassed.

My guide also told me about some of the local plants. Breaking a leaf from one, he showed me its milky sap and said, 'It's poison. Very bad.' I was interested. Apparently all you had to do was stir the unwanted husband's cup of tea with this leaf and you could be down at the Social Security Office collecting your widow's pension just as fast as you could say, 'Drink up your tea dear, before it gets cold.'

Back at the Bush Haus it was the 'grandmere of the babee' and the manager's wife who did the cooking and meals were taken communally. I loved eating in the open air above the darkening water, especially when a cheeky dwarf species of lemur visited us. He obviously felt perfectly entitled to help himself to any fruit he fancied. Orphaned as a baby, he had been reared by the Bush Haus owners and still considered himself one of the family, popping in nightly for a handout. There was a rush to hide the fruit bowls to prevent his making off with the lot. He jumped onto my table, grabbed a banana and sat down to eat it leisurely in front of me.

I had a marvellous sleep in another four-poster, this one so huge it filled the small hut. The quiet was wonderful and, except for the forest noises, absolute. Here there was no phone, or television, and the electricity, supplied by a generator, only worked from five in the evening till ten. After that, it was candles for illumination, but by that time I was long asleep.

I woke yet again to the sound of heavy rain, but not until half-past-five. Throwing open the wooden shutters of my hut, there was the forest – dripping, washed clean, and luscious. After another great breakfast and a chat to the German students, I farewelled the Bush Haus and set off in their boat for Manombato, on the coast.

This was a pleasant ride across the lake and down the canal, made more so by the usual extreme courtesy people showed to each other on the waterways. Motorboats slowed down for even the smallest canoe and never passed another craft without a greeting. They moved respectfully through fish traps, not wanting to damage someone else's means of earning a living. Once again I noted how little habitation there was and how much wilderness.

Manombato is a tiny, obscure fishing village and it doesn't run to a boat landing. I had to jump overboard and splash ashore from several metres out. There was no car either. The village was quite a way from the beach, which was absolutely bare. The arrangements for my onward travel had been rather vague, but the driver of the boat had been instructed not to abandon me without help. Eventually a village man came by and I was passed on to him for safekeeping. He and I sat down under a bush to wait.

After about an hour a Toyota Land Cruiser arrived with two travellers seeking the Bush Haus. My keeper negotiated with the car's driver, who agreed to take me on to Brickaville where I hoped to connect with Madabus.

I had been told that it was seven kilometres from the beach

to the road that led to Brickaville. I found this hard to believe. It seemed thousands! It took forty-five minutes to cross that abominable sand track. We crawled up and down almost perpendicular hills, lurching from one hole to another and crashing in and out of deep ruts. Finally we found the road, and ten kilometres later I arrived in Brickaville.

Then the fun started. My driver, not unnaturally, wanted to offload me. He asked many people for directions but no one had ever heard of a bus. He tried several times to leave me at likely places, but I refused to be left. So far he hadn't hit the spot I remembered Madabus waiting to collect travellers when I had been on my way north to Toamasina. I wasn't sure, but I hoped this might be also where the bus would stop when going in the opposite direction.

Finally I saw a cafe that I thought was the place. Several people sat at tables on the pavement in front of it, including a Frenchman and his driver. I asked everyone, patrons and staff, about the bus, in English and French (or so I imagined). It was a dead loss. No one understood me. The Frenchman had a little English, but it was somewhat impeded by his having just recently drunk his lunch. Surrounded by empty beer and wine bottles, he was red in the face and laughed a lot. That applied to me too by now. I find smiling a lot helps in this kind of situation.

Eventually I managed to get through to Monsieur that I wanted to know if the bus stopped here. He asked the three staff members. They vigorously denied ever having heard of any bus. And yet I was positive that in my earlier trip we had been parked in front of this place for an hour. The bus was big and green – you could hardly have missed it. But just because it had stopped there on the way up, didn't mean that it would stop there coming back. I had learned from past encounters with buses that they can be extraordinarily contrary in such matters and I no longer trust them.

Meanwhile, my driver, still trying to detach himself from

me, was also making wide enquiries. The gendarme across the road said, '*Oui, oui*, the bus comes here but it stops up the road a kilometre.'

The other patrons gave answers – about fifteen different ones, and not one of them definite. And none of them said the bus stopped at this place except one inventive chap who informed us it arrived at four in the morning. I even had the assistance of two men working on road repairs who came over to join in the fun. They were from Malaysia and spoke English. They didn't know anything about the bus, but at least they understood what I was going on about. Most of the participants in the ensuing argument wanted to send me to the *taxi brousse* station in the village two kilometres away.

Then a bus appeared on the road and they all rushed out to shout and wave it down. It wasn't Madabus, but the driver added his bit to the confusion by saying that, yes, he knew Madabus. He had passed it ten kilometres back and it would stop at the *hotely* I could see in the distance. An hour later it hadn't appeared. Another Frenchman came. He asked Madame, the proprietor, who, having previously denied all knowledge of any bus, now said, 'Yes, it comes at two-thirty.'

And it did! At half-past-two, almost on the dot, there, much to everyone's relief, was Madabus. I was given a great send off, and the inebriated Frenchman insisted on paying for my coffee. It had taken fifteen people to catch a bus for me.

I was the only passenger on the bus for the five-and-a-half hour ride to Tana. Halfway there we stopped and the driver turned to me and said, 'Pee pee.' Obediently I did as ordered, hiding among the shrubbery by the roadside. Coming into Tana at eight o'clock, I looked into the dark night as we drove along the narrow streets and saw the *hotelys* and stalls standing in yellow pools of light given off by kerosene lanterns. There was no refrigeration here and meat that had lain all day in the open air remained on the wooden counters of the butchers' stalls, kept company by swinging ropes of sausages.

I took a taxi to the Shanghai. '*Je reviens*,' I said gleefully as I arrived. Which I hoped was, 'I have returned.' It was the name of a perfume I once had. Whatever. They could see I was back no matter what it meant.

In the morning, when it was time to go to the airport for my flight to Mauritius, I said a sad goodbye to the friendly staff at the Shanghai. The receptionist gave me the three kisses I'd now got the hang of as I climbed into the taxi. The road to the airport looked nowhere near as dreary to me now as it had on my arrival. Funny how you get used to things. Flying here from Italy had been an all-night effort, so I guess I hadn't felt disposed to be kind to Tana.

As we flew out I looked down to say farewell to Madagascar. My visit had been a happy one and I was taking away good memories.

So here I was flying with Mad Air. Not something I had looked forward to with relish. Although my ticket with Air Mauritius gave me a flight to Madagascar with that airline, I had not been told that you have to fly Air Madagascar to leave the country. But the hostesses in their short-skirted red suits were very smart, the steward was handsome in the extreme, and they were all very obliging. The food was excellent and, although there was a lot of bumping due to the cumulus cloud hanging about, we landed safely. It turned out to be the sensational food that nearly killed me. If given the choice, though, I guess I would opt for food poisoning rather than an air crash.

Standing in the aisle next to me in the immigration line I spotted the manager of the Bank of Africa, the man in Tana I had forced to cash my traveller's cheques. I could not have missed him, with his full-moon face like a frying pan with a couple of eggs stuck to it and a bulldog jaw. I wondered if I should say hello. The assistant manager, who had been so charming to me, was with him. But, I thought, what if they think I am skipping out of Madagascar having cashed all my bad cheques. But then again, were they the ones doing the skipping? It seemed strange they were both leaving the country at the same time – absconding with the bank's funds maybe?

Despite my fiscal purity, all was not a breeze for me at immigration. Entry to Mauritius does not require Australians to have a visa and I got through customs easily, but at the immigration desk my sin was discovered. I hadn't written where I would be staying on my form. Officialdom apparently is not used to travellers who are not with a tour group. The officer insisted I supply the name of a hotel. I got out my guidebook and furnished him with one. He gave me a suspicious look. Unfortunately, not having my glasses on, I had picked a restaurant. I chose another and he finally let me through.

But I had not escaped yet. At the exit of the immigration hall two stern-faced officers waited. They singled me out of the crowd and stopped me.

'Where are you staying,' one demanded.

I rattled off the name I had chosen. 'The Canton in Port Louis.'

'Was that the hotel name you gave at the desk?'

'Yes,' I said.

'Where is your onward ticket?'

I rummaged in my bag and found the ticket. He showed it to another officer and they had a conference.

'When do you leave?'

It's on the ticket, dum dum, I managed to restrain myself from shouting. More questions followed. Eventually I got away.

A young French couple came up to me laughing. 'That happened to us when we came here before,' they said.

The officers had made the bloke leave the woman with them as a hostage, while he went out to the hotel-booking desk in the airport foyer and booked a room.

Oh, well. I had made it. Ten days in Mauritius, here I come.

19 The Wrong Mr Right

Mauritius, or Maurice to give it its French name, was not what I had expected. Perhaps I had been anticipating more of Madagascar, which I had liked very much, but this was remarkably different.

I stepped, with relief at my escape from the Tourist Gestapo, out of the airport building and into a moist, tropical atmosphere tempered by a breeze. The airport grounds were filled with groomed gardens of palms, trees and flowers. It was all so green and clean.

I climbed effortlessly into a taxi without the skirmish I had become accustomed to recently. My second surprise was the car. Late model, air-conditioned, with no rattles and clangs. I could have been in a taxi at home. Not that I expect the comforts of home when travelling. It was just a bonus.

As I waited for my bag I had decided against staying in the capital, Port Louis, and chosen to venture to Mahébourg, a town on the south-east coast. Reading the map I had realised that Port Louis was on the other side of the island from the airport, and it seemed a better plan to start with the nearest town. The lovely twenty-minute ride to reach it traversed a green, green landscape; everywhere I looked there were large fields of sugar cane and rice paddy, and a general feeling of neatness and prosperity.

I was well on the way to Mahébourg before I released with a jolt that I had lied to Immigration! What if they checked up on me and found I wasn't in Port Louis? They had seemed convinced that I was the sort of delinquent, of no fixed abode, likely to skip off, visa-less, to end my days beachcombing and being an embarrassment to the government.

My taxidriver was an older man of Indian appearance. He said that he regretted the loss of British rule in 1968. 'Life was more orderly then,' he said, 'you knew what was what.' He talked all the way to Mahébourg after I had asked if he spoke English. I won't do that again. He seemed affronted, as though I had asked him if he was illiterate.

Reading my guidebook in the taxi I discovered that I had committed another felony. The Canton, which I had given Immigration as my second choice of hotel, was in fact another restaurant. Oh dear. Now I really worried. I had doubly misled them. And those severe gents who had interrogated me didn't seem the kind to laugh off a couple of innocent mistakes. They had been deeply distrustful of my motives.

The taxidriver took me to a guesthouse that he said was a good place to stay, adding that if I didn't fancy it he would take me elsewhere. I liked the guesthouse but said it was too dear. The price immediately fell almost half, and I took the room. Mauritius is not an expensive place to visit, but it is not the bargain that Madagascar is. The Mauritian rupee is about twenty to one Australian dollar. The young manager took my passport, saying that she had to go and register me with the police. Help! It got worse. An immigration check would reveal not only that I had said I was going to stay in a fictitious residence, but that I had absconded to another town, which would surely confirm their worst fears about me.

But right then I felt an urgent need to take to my couch. All was not entirely brilliant in my stomach regions. After an hour I got up to be thoroughly sick. Later I did it again. And again. The Mad Air food had caught up with me.

I took a couple of food-poison antidote pills and finally slept, but then I couldn't wake up in the morning. I didn't surface until four in the afternoon, shaky, but still alive. The manager had knocked on my door at ten in the morning and asked why I hadn't fronted for breakfast. When I said that I was ill, she offered to bring food to me. 'No thanks,' I countered. The mention of food had caused a rebellion in my gastrointestinal tract.

'Then you call me if you want anything, Madame,' she said.

By evening I was semi-restored enough to notice that my place of residence, the Coco Villa Guesthouse, had an absolute sea frontage. Three storeys high, its rooms had semi-circular, Romeo and Juliet balconies, while at ground level there were patios set on a lawn a few steps from the sea wall. I walked up the street for some yoghurt, the only thing my internal workings did not go into armed revolt at the thought of.

Next morning I pronounced myself cured and couldn't wait for breakfast. To miss one meal is a serious matter for me, two and it is almost time to call the ambulance. The hotel's cheery, yellow and blue seafront cafe even ran to cheese – if you can call those little cream-cheese triangles 'cheese' – and the big coffeepot helped in my recovery. It was good coffee, strong like that of Madagascar.

I set off slowly, gathering speed as the day wore on. Investigating my surroundings, I learned the French had founded Mahébourg as a port in 1805. I also discovered Mauritius had been under colonial rule of one kind or another for nearly 400 years. Everyone seemed to have had a hand in it. The island was uninhabited until 1598 when Dutch seafarers established a supply base on the south-east coast for ships en route to Batavia (Jakarta). They named the island Mauritius – after Prince Maurice van Nassau, the *Stadthouder* (governor) of the Netherlands – but abandoned it in 1710 after exterminating the dodo and introducing African slaves, sugar cane, deer and tobacco. Next came the French, who called the place Ile de France, and stayed until they were ousted by the English in 1810. Both colonial powers established economies based on slave-worked sugar plantations. The British remained until independence in 1968, and since then a democratic government has been in place. The current prime minister is Paul Berenger, the country's first non-Indian to hold the post.

I ambled along Mahébourg's pretty esplanade, enjoying its neat lawns, flowers, and banyan and poinciana trees. Leaving the seafront, I entered the quiet, tree-lined residential streets. This was another town that I immediately liked. Once a busy port, Mahébourg is now a sleepy home to the local fishing fleet.

I found a naval museum behind some commanding gates at the end of a driveway, shaded by big trees and surrounded by a forest of cool pines. The museum housed many maps and relics from shipwrecks, as well as the story of the island's history and its immigration. I spent an enjoyable hour here and learned that the Mauritians are an ethnic mix of Indian, Chinese, Creole and French origin. The Indians are descended from indentured workers brought here for work on the cane fields; the Creoles from African slaves and Europeans; and the Chinese from migrants who came as self-employed entrepreneurs. Most banks, sugar mills and other big business are still owned by Franco-Mauritians, the descendents of white settlers.

Walking on down the road back toward the shore, past the lemon-coloured Catholic cathedral with its lofty tower, I came to the market. All the women, from young girls to old ladies, carried sunshades. I felt quite at home. There were no asinine comments here like, 'Hey lady, its not raining!' from ignorant drongos who don't have the sense to get out of the sun. An umbrella that keeps you twenty degrees cooler makes a big difference to how long you can walk.

The women were not afraid of colour. Many wore fabulously hued saris, which I consider to be the most becoming thing a woman can wear. Some were dressed in the second most flattering outfit, the Punjabi suit, a long blouse worn with matching pants and scarf, the latter draped gracefully over one or both shoulders. There were also Muslim women in long dresses and *hijabs*. I saw only one woman in a black *abeya* and headscarf.

Evidence of the various religions was everywhere. Half the population is Hindu, one-fifth Muslim, and one-third Catholic – but among the Creoles, Christianity is mixed with voodoo. All the religions exist side by side in tolerance. I had woken this morning to the sound of the *mezzuin* calling the faithful to prayer; and moving from one house to the next I would pass a shrine to the Virgin Mary rubbing shoulders with that of the Indian saint in the neighbour's yard.

This was an orderly town, heaped with civic pride and a feeling of prosperity. Even in the back streets there was almost no litter. Women were busy sweeping the pavements in front of their houses. There were some poor-looking houses but nothing like the hovels in Madagascar. Mauritius has a stable government, a thriving economy and a positive human rights record.

The market was also spruce and clean. Housed in a solid green and white building, it boasted an office labelled 'Inspector of Health'. From the market I wandered into more back streets and eventually found myself in a lane only big enough for the police car and me. The police car! Nervously I slid past, convinced that the four solid, uniformed Upholders of the Law were scrutinising me. It shows what a guilty conscience can do to you.

At five o'clock, after siesta, I set off again. This time I followed the waterfront around to the main street. It was Sunday and Mahébourg was dead by evening – everything was shut, few souls were about, and there was little traffic. I walked by the Nice Place Guesthouse and entered a small back lane, pausing to watch groups of men playing cards or board games. In a park boys kicked a soccer ball while two men reclined on the grass with a picnic spread between them, bottles of beer and plastic containers of food. More men played cards sitting on a pile of rocks. There were many dogs but no strays, and I saw a few well-fed cats. Even the sparrows seemed festive – they were orange here.

At a tiny one-man cafe on the foreshore I ate Fish Creole, a scrumptious local dish. The friendly cook shook my hand when I left and wished me *bon voyage*.

While I ate I heard a voice I recognised. I had not thought it possible that anyone really spoke like that, but here was Julian Clary in real life, hand gestures, eye rollings, sibilant sses, the lot. The act was so camp I thought he had to be joking but no, he seemed for real. I had to refrain from looking at this apparition to avoid bursting out laughing. The cook commendably managed to keep a straight face, although he did seem a little bemused. He sat this customer inside and not out on the footpath with me, perhaps thinking he might not be as good an advertisement as I was.

The next morning I decided it was time to move on to Port Louis. There is no bus and the two-hour ride is done by taxi. Mauritius is a small island in which 1.2 million souls are packed onto 2000-odd square kilometres of land.

I asked Madame of the guesthouse if she could recommend a driver. A big mistake. A young Indian of the spiv persuasion materialised. I recognised the type. He proceeded to quote me a ridiculous price and insisted that I needed to take in prodigious amounts of shopping and meals en route. After a lot of haggling I agreed to a price I knew was too much, but it suited me. I wanted to go via Cap Baia to pay my respects to Matthew Flinders. I must have still been in a weakened state, otherwise I would have had the courage to back out when this dodgy character, henceforth known as the Sharp Operator, kept trying to make me agree to visit shops. Whatever. I do silly things sometimes for a quiet life. If I had known what a terrible driver he was, though, the deal would not have been on.

We roared off at 1000 kilometres an hour down the small streets. The car was a smart new Toyota, but the driver continually jerked the wheel sideways, lurching it around corners. And his foot repeatedly stabbed hard at the brake pedal. We sped, lurched and jerked our way down the coast to Blue Bay – which it certainly was. Although the sea was not separated from the lagoon, there was a clear line of demarcation and the colour of the lagoon was dramatically different from that of the sea, a pure turquoise while the sea was dark indigo blue. Graceful casuarinas shaded the Blue Bay foreshore, which had grass right to the water's edge, and the village behind was pretty.

From Blue Bay we continued inland for a while, past enormous tracts of sugar cane in the midst of which a couple of sugar mills belched thick plumes of black smoke. It was harvest time and great beasts of mechanical harvesters tramped through the fields. Although much cane had been cut, some still stood tall and green, creating a terrain of unbelievable lushness. Riding between the fields that lined the road, I felt as though the whole world had turned green. The cane was watered by overhead sprinklers, either big jet sprays or mobile units that crept along a line at a time. There were also banana and mango trees, riotously flowering purple, red and white bougainvillea, and many other flowers.

Mauritius is the peak of an enormous undersea volcanic chain and the flat coastal land soon climbed to a lofty plateau. We passed through a couple of moderately large towns, but I was surprised to find large stretches of the interior free of people or houses. Halfway across the island we turned and took the road that led back to the coast, following this road to its southern end.

Along the coast we passed Green Bay, where another lagoon contrasted with the darker colour of the sea. This lagoon was a light green, a hybrid of aquamarine and peridot. I enjoyed the lovely scenery, despite the haste with which we rocketed through the narrow streets of the villages.

Outside the village of Bel Ombre a Christian cemetery stood on a stretch of bare sand hill, right on the beachfront, and all the crosses on the graves faced the sea. I couldn't help thinking that the spirits had a grand outlook. Now and then I saw the tomb of an ancestor who had been planted among his rice or cane fields. You can't take it with you, but here at least you could stay with it. Low, square, colourfully painted stone structures, the tombs were both Christian and other religions.

Large stretches of this part of the coast were also bare of habitation and the settlements that do exist, consist of smart beach houses scattered along the shore. In many places forests of pines ran right to the water's edge. Some of the coastline was wonderfully wild. Here the sea rolled in in large breakers onto lonely white sand beaches, fringed with spreading casuarinas sighing in the wind that whipped the surf.

At Cap Baie I found what I had come this way seeking – Matthew Flinders's monument. I was making a pilgrimage to a hero of my childhood. All South Australian schoolchildren of my era were taught to admire this master mariner's epic voyages of discovery and his charting of Australia's unknown waters and coastline. And it was Matthew who gave us our name, Australia. How much nicer to be an Australian than to have to trot around the world claiming to be a Terra Australis Incognitian.

In his own lifetime, poor Matthew Flinders failed to win recognition for his great work, due to the fact that he had spent six years as a prisoner in Mauritius. In 1803 he was on his way back to England with the charts for which he would have received fame and fortune when, in need of repairs to his ship, he had come ashore at this spot, Cap Baie, and been arrested by the French. Unbeknownst to him, war had broken out between England and France. Back in England, at only forty years of age, he died the day after his book was published.

Impressive and grand, Matthew Flinders' monument is a bronze sculpture depicting him with his cat, Trim, the faithful companion who had sailed with him since he first left England. Erected in 2003 on the 200th anniversary of his landing here, the monument stands just above the shore on a lovely, lonely headland looking out to the ocean, as befits a man of the sea. I hope Flinders knows that now and then an Australian will come to pay homage to him. He inspired me as a child and possibly created this urge I have to travel the world by ship.

Matthew Flinders has not been forgotten in Mauritius. There is another, older monument on the site of his confinement. Later, in the Port Louis bookshop, I was able to buy a book that tells the story of his six years of imprisonment, *In the grips of the eagle*, by Huguette Ly-Tio-Fane Pineo.

From Cap Baie the Sharp Operator – he tried all along the way to entice me to go shopping – and I proceeded north up the coast to Port Louis. I had travelled more than halfway around the entire island in three hours, admittedly, at the speed of light.

The approach to Port Louis was not encouraging. Its outlying sprawl is dirty, smoggy and polluted. The driver made one last attempt to lure me into a shop, but I refused to be lured, even when he said he wanted to buy me a present. Oh yeah. At one stage of the journey he had stopped to phone the hotel I was heading for. He didn't ask for directions, but rather tried to screw a commission from them. It wasn't until he had followed me up the stairs and into the hotel for one more shot at getting a kickback from the staff that I finally got rid of Mr Sharp Operator.

Later Mr Wong, the hotel owner/manager, confirmed this.

'I hope you didn't pay him,' I said.

'Not bloody likely!' Mr Wong replied – or Chinese words to that effect.

20 Home

At first I was dismayed by the appearance of the Bourbon Tourist Hotel. It skulked in a rather scruffy street of Chinatown, above a collection of small shops. In fact, at times after hours, I felt as though I was alone in a warehouse. The place had a deserted feel about it; I saw no other inhabitant for the first day and night. Access to the hotel was down a long, dark passage between the shops and up two flights of stairs, at the top of which was the entrance, barred by an iron grille and then a gate.

But on arrival a smiling Mr Wong came to meet me and escort me to my room. My genial host assured me that he would take good care of me and that my belongings and I were safe in his establishment.

'Anything you want I will do,' he beamed.

My room was big and looked superficially clean. Decorated in the Soviet utilitarian style, it reminded me of the cheap Chinese hotels of Singapore and Hong Kong. I scrubbed the hand basin with toilet paper and soap, lined the shelf with more paper, and only then felt it was safe to put my toothbrush down.

Mr Wong obligingly offered to make me some lunch. Fried rice and chop suey.

After eating, I ventured out. How different the downtown part of Port Louis was after the impression I had gained from its outskirts. The waterfront has been developed as a tourist attraction and it had certainly worked. The place was crawling with tourists everywhere I looked. And the shops and buildings were oh so posh. Until 1970 the sugar industry provided ninety per cent of Mauritius's income and employment, but tourism and textiles have now replaced sugar as the island's major earner. By the 1990s Mauritius had become one of the world's largest exporters of textiles, and famous brands like Ralph Lauren and Pierre Cardin began manufacturing here. Unemployment fell and living standards rose for Port Louis' 170,000 inhabitants as visitors flocked in to enjoy beach resorts and shops full of the latest fashions. There were some wonderful goods in the shops at some pretty wonderful prices, but I left them there.

The waterfront even ran to a public toilet, with three uniformed attendants, no less. The smart toilet paper holder featured a brass padlock to stop people pinching the roll, but there was no paper. The toilet paper holder had been outsmarted.

The internet worked in the cafe I stopped at and phone cards did too, which made my day. Then I went walking.

I noticed more women wearing *purdah* here and it was the whole kit and caboodle, everything covered except their eyes. By the end of the day when my hair was standing on end and I looked like the dog's breakfast, I wished I could wear it too.

The Dutch first settled Port Louis in the seventeenth century but it remained a minor settlement until, in 1736, the French, under Governor Labourdonnais, made it into a port and the country's capital. Today a grand statue of Labourdonnais stands on an imposing position at the sea-end of the attractive, tree-framed main square, which runs from the harbour to the lovely, colonial government house. Built in 1738 by the French, the government house is still in use today, guarded by a statue of Queen Victoria.

I walked for hours, long after everything was shut, until I was wandering aimlessly in the back streets of Chinatown, having somehow misplaced my residence. There was still a lot of activity on the streets. The rubbish, which was tossed from the shops into the gutter at the end of the day, was being sorted and stacked, by men wearing big gauntlet gloves, ready for the truck that went around collecting it.

A man passed me. '*Bon soir,*' he said and then turning added, 'Watch out for your bug.'

'Thanks,' I said, 'I will.' And for my bag too.

Two streets further on another man called to me from a balcony, from where he probably had been watching me wander around in circles for some time.

'Where do you want to go?'

I told him and he gave me directions, and I soon came to rest where I belonged.

Breakfast was included in my room price. My bread and coffee appeared, carried by a lumpy middle-aged Indian woman in a baggy red dress, her arrival announced long before she was in view by the slop-slop of her slippers on the tiled floor. A cool breeze blew into the wide aisle between the rooms where I sat at a small table for breakfast. While I munched the terrific crusty bread they make in Mauritius, I listened to Mr Wong's collection of caged budgies and canaries that he kept on the veranda at the end of the aisle, along with the washing and other miscellany. He came to feed his birds each morning, talking lovingly to them all the while. I hate to see anything caged and contemplated setting them free when he wasn't looking, but decided they might be worse off out there in the big, bad world.

Before he arrived, the wild pigeons, ever on the look out for a freebee, swooped in to pinch the cloistered ones' bread, which had been left unattended in a bucket. One pigeon performed the ritual-courting dance in front of a female. She finished eating and flew away, but by then he was on autopilot and kept on dancing without noticing that she had left the scene. It reminded me of the sights you see in a disco.

In my Mauritius guidebook I read that you could take a submarine ride down to a depth of thirty-five metres at Grand Baie, thirty kilometres up the coast from Port Louis. Why not, I thought, momentarily forgetting my claustrophobic tendencies, and I set off in a taxi to give it a try. It takes twenty minutes in a taxi or an hour in a local bus to reach the northern beaches. The coast is fairly built-up and there were only a few patches of cultivation. This was lotus land, the land of the tourist. Like the waterfront, it was not my scene at all.

I found the submarine place, booked in, then went for a reconnoitre. The hotel across the way was a deluxe model and their loo was sublime. It even had unlocked toilet paper.

Later I met my fellow divers and we received our instructions. The other valiant five were English tourists, some of them nervous. A young couple told me they were on their honeymoon. Introducing me to their older companion, I realised he was the young bloke's dad.

'You brought your father on your honeymoon!' I asked, astonished. 'Was that for moral support or back up?'

But they explained that they had been married here in Mauritius. What a good idea. Beats all the hassle of a wedding at home with the 200 rellies you have to ask but don't want to.

We clambered into a launch and made our way out to the mother ship, which was anchored in the harbour. The sea was choppy, but we managed to transfer to our vessel without mishaps. Then we stepped down backwards, one at a time, into the submarine that was fastened alongside. We were sealed into this small, anxiety-inducing phial and it descended to a depth of thirty-four metres and stayed there for an hour (I have a certificate to prove it). The sub was clear Perspex all around and, I am happy to say, we had a pilot.

Once the initial jitters caused by being locked in a see-through coffin subsided, we were too busy marvelling at the novelty of floating noiselessly under the sea to worry any more. We saw a lionfish and many other sea creatures at close range as we travelled along the edge of a coral reef. As we ascended again we were surrounded by millions of bubbles, as if we sat in a boiling kettle. After we had resurfaced and decompressed our ears, we hopped out and climbed over to the mother ship for a drink before transferring back to shore.

After my adventure I caught a bus to return to Port Louis. Now that I had the hang of bus travel there would be no stopping me. It was dirt-cheap and you can see everything from up high. And even though it was a rickety old jalopy and the driver had racetrack yearnings, I felt safe. Once the driver swerved in under a roadside tree and the conductor leaned out to snatch a raffia basket that contained his lunch from where it had been hooked over a branch.

Back at the hotel Mr Wong greeted me like the returning prodigal, eager to hear about my adventure under the sea. When I said that tomorrow I was going to see about buying some gold bangles like the Indian women wear, he told me that he would show me some.

After the first day I had company in the hotel. The group was Chinese and all male. They regarded me as a curiosity but, although taken aback at first when I made an appearance, these blokes, who seemed to be mostly small businessmen, were always courteous. Except for breakfast, the hotel did not provide meals, so in the evening I ate down the street at a restaurant Mr Wong recommended. It was grand of décor, but I dined alone except for a surly waiter who seemed to disapprove of me. The food was only fair and when I ordered vegetables I got a bucketful of horrible green weeds. And they charged an exorbitant price for water.

After a night or two, walking back from dinner up the

street that was, by then, deserted except for men unloading stores for the shops, I was now recognised and greetings were called to me. I think tourists were rare in this quarter, most come for the resorts, few stay in Chinatown – a lone Western female was even rarer.

Mr Wong kept his promise to show me some bangles. I had presumed that he knew someone with a shop, but to my astonishment he took me to a bank. The bangles were his. I have never been in a bank vault before and it was a rather queer experience. Once inside the building we went down a flight of steps that took us into the bowels of the earth. The keeper of the vault knew Mr Wong well. Goodness knows what else he had squirreled away in there. The family jewels for a start. He signed in through a cubbyhole in a counter and then he and I were admitted to the inner sanctum. I was left there, seated on a chair, while he went into the vault, after it had been unlocked for him.

Mr Wong was gone for quite some time, and then came out with a box. Meanwhile I'd had plenty of time to plan a little wickedness. Mr Wong was well known to the staff but I could have been a crook for all they knew. I could have followed him in, bopped him on the head, and nipped off with the booty before they realised it. They had left the door open.

After all this excitement I didn't like his bangles enough to buy them. But I left with an amethyst ring he had insisted I put on and wear. Did this mean we were engaged? I hoped not. He had made a point of establishing the fact that he was single, semi-retired, and well off. But, although he was a fine fellow, he was not Mr Right; he was – the story of my life – the Chinese version, Mr Wong!

Then Mr Wong took me to a jeweller's shop where I did find some bangles I liked and I bought them. After this I took off on my own after breaking our engagement by forcing the amethyst ring back on him.

I discovered the market was a ghastly tourist trap, a nightmare of hustlers, and I ended up zipping through it at a fast trot. Seeking refuge in a cafe, I caused a domestic dispute of quite some calibre after I asked for black coffee without sugar, one French phrase I usually have no trouble with. The husband told the wife to get it, but a problem of some kind ensued and much shouting took place. This cafe seemed to be an all-male hangout and the men at the other tables laughed heartily at this row. They were drinking large bottles of beer at ten o'clock in the morning. I would have been laughing too if I'd had an infusion of alcohol at that hour.

Making use of my newfound knowledge of bus travel, I went to the bus station, intent on getting to the Lourdes of the Indian Ocean, the shrine of Pere Laval. A French missionary priest, he died in 1864 and was beatified in 1979 by Pope John Paul II. There have been numerous miracles credited to visits to his tomb. Pilgrims come from as far away as Africa, Britain and France and locals of all religions go there to pray. Why not me? A free shot at a miracle is not to be sneezed at.

After circumnavigating the entire bus station with no success, I asked a conductor where the right bus was to be found. He directed me to a sign that declared 'Pere Laval', and I waited patiently beside it until a bus came along. But when I asked the driver for confirmation of his destination he denied this. 'No,' he said, 'Ici,' pointing to another post three lanes over.

In the fullness of time I was shunted onto the right bus. The bus, loaded to full capacity and complete with a screaming baby, took off. I hoped the baby would be cured of whatever ailed it at the shrine and had shut up by the return trip. Fifteen minutes later I climbed off at the terminus. I walked about. No shrine. I asked a woman in a small shop its whereabouts and she told me that I had come too far.

Returning to the bus, which still stood at the terminus, I told the conductor I had to return. Not with him apparently.

He took me to another bus waiting nearby, telling its driver to put me off at the right place and not to charge me for another ticket. I accepted this placidly. I hadn't really expected to get there at my first attempt. The miracles occur after the shrine, not before.

The shrine is housed in a small building on one side of a large modern church. Inside, the faithful surrounded a bier on which a painted plaster statue of Pere Laval lay, looking exceedingly saintly under his glass cover. My fellow pilgrims numbered about a dozen, men and women of all persuasions – Indians in saris, Chinese in pantsuits and Western dress. They placed candles and flowers on the glass covering the saint, and then rubbed their hands over any part of the bier they could reach and smoothed them over their heads and hearts. One old woman was crying. Parents were blessing children. No one made a sound. They just stood there absorbed in silent prayer. I joined them and after a while I did the blessing bit too. It doesn't hurt to hedge your bets. And if my dodgy back – I once foolishly took part in a car rally in a vehicle that eventually rolled – was cured the next day I would sprint to join the flock of Mother Church. My second pilgrimage completed I continued on my way.

My days on this journey were running out, and I was looking forward to going home. I had been living out of a suitcase for nearly three months.

Early one morning I set off to explore the commercial part of Chinatown. After the big build-up of the grand Friendship gates over the street that mark its entrance, it was a total flop – shop after shop of electrical fittings in one street and another with taps, plumbing and bathroom stuff galore. I wondered whatever the need for all those were. A testimony to Mauritius's cultural harmony, beside the Friendship gates was the city's huge, arresting mosque. A large white and green building, it had cake-icing scallops all around it and was topped by a gold dome from whence issued the call to prayer. Beneath the dome a green flag with the symbol of Islam, the star and sickle moon, fluttered.

Frustrated in my search for Chinese goods in Chinatown, I went to the museum. This handsome old building contained some fascinating collections and I spent a long time examining birds, shells and fish and, of course, the legendary dodo (the only complete example in the world resides here). I secretly thought it looked exceedingly stupid. No wonder it had become extinct if it had had no more sense than to run joyously to meet a lot of hungry sailors.

Walking on I found many more interesting buildings including the grim, fortress-like church of St Luis, where I popped in to lodge a quick word of complaint. To my disappointment I had not leapt up rejoicing this morning with a cured back. I thought a bit of a top-up might help.

I was sitting on the waterfront tucking into a *halaal* meal when a dapper young man in a suit asked if he could join me. He told me he was a jockey.

'Put that beer down at once you naughty boy,' I said.

But he just laughed and replied his weight was fine. My new friend reminded me that the Melbourne Cup would be run in a few days time, adding that he had aspirations to come to it one day. He asked if he could take me to the races the next day, Saturday. Regretfully I had to decline. Tomorrow I planned to be flying across the Indian Ocean home to Australia.

I had to move on: the meaning of life awaits!

Also by Lydia Laube

BEHIND THE VEIL
THE LONG WAY HOME
SLOW BOAT TO MONGOLIA
BOUND FOR VIETNAM
LLAMA FOR LUNCH
TEMPLES & TUK TUKS
LOST IN LAOS
FROM BURMA TO MYANMAR

Wakefield Press is an independent publishing and
distribution company based in Adelaide, South Australia.
We love good stories and publish beautiful books.
To see our full range of books, please visit our website at
www.wakefieldpress.com.au
where all titles are available for purchase.
To keep up with our latest releases, news and events,
subscribe to our monthly newsletter.

Find us!

Facebook: www.facebook.com/wakefield.press
Twitter: www.twitter.com/wakefieldpress
Instagram: www.instagram.com/wakefieldpress

www.ingramcontent.com/pod-product-compliance
Lightning Source LLC
Chambersburg PA
CBHW031954080426
42735CB00007B/388